Art, Architecture, Fashion:
Vintage Akris in a Brutalist Gesamtkunstwerk

By Roland Wäspe

In certain magical places, extraordinary events unfold over decades that later go down in history as outstanding cultural achievements. One such place is the University of St. Gallen (HSG) with its now world-famous business school, which in 1963 opened a new building designed by architect Walter M. Förderer.

St. Gallen was going through a phase of dramatic changes. The ensemble that made up Switzerland's first pioneering campus university was aptly named "La Tête," as it was intended that it should represent precisely this: it would stand for the intellectual head of the city.

Classical Modernism had arrived in St. Gallen. Today, the projects initiated by Eduard Naegeli, the president of the Kunstverein St. Gallen (St. Gallen Art Association) are regarded as outstanding examples of the interplay between architecture and the fine arts. This begins outside the building when one sees a rhythmic group of eleven concrete sculptures by Alicia Penalba, before pausing in front of a small water basin with the organically shaped bronze *Schalenbaum* by Hans Arp. A ceramic frieze by Joan Miró and ceramicist Josep Llorens Artigas runs around the foyer, while three lead panels by Étienne Hajdú with organic motifs in relief form a spatial framing. A gray cubic relief by Basel painter Soniatta, so subtle you could almost miss it, hangs from the ceiling, affording a view to its right of a wall-based mosaic by Georges Braque with the motif from the color etching *Oiseau.*

Suspended above the central open staircase, a mobile by Alexander Calder underscores its lightness and dynamism. On the second floor, the space opens up, offering vistas of the surrounding park and cityscape. With its broad black brushstrokes, a large raw yarn tapestry by Pierre Soulages conjures up a special sense of calm and security in this corner of the building, complete with comfortable seating. At the end of the narrow stairway to the library, on the second floor, a bronze figure by Alberto Giacometti, *Stehende (Standing Woman),* just 59 centimeters high, is strikingly illuminated thanks to a skylight.

It is not simply the outstanding quality of the commissioned works that makes this fusion of architecture and fine arts so significant, but also the overarching conceptual idea that creates unique synergies between the building, the art and the users. Classical Modernism was based on the belief that society could be refined through daily encounters with art. Setting Albert Kriemler's models in this context weaves them into this tradition.

Previous pages and next page: Iwan Baan photographed
original pieces designed by Albert Kriemler for Akris
from 1979 to 1992 in the Brutalist landmark that is the main
building of the University of St. Gallen

Akris – A Century in Fashion

selbstverständlich

Edited by
Albert Kriemler and Peter Kriemler

With contributions by
Daniel Binswanger
Jessica Iredale
John Neumeier
Nicole Phelps
Anne Urbauer
Nicole Urbschat
Roland Wäspe

Photo essays by
Iwan Baan

Lars Müller Publishers

Table of Contents

Introduction

By Nicole Phelps

I remember meeting Albert Kriemler backstage at his Fall/Winter 2013 Akris show. He and his brother Peter who runs the business side of the house had recently lost their mother Ute, and they were both emotional. The collection was a tribute to her: all in black and inspired by her personal wardrobe of turtleneck gowns, blouse-and-pant sets, and clean tailoring. Akris is called a minimalist's collection by just about everyone, but that definition ignores its soul. It's also a family affair, deeply rooted in its hometown of St. Gallen in Switzerland, and informed by its earliest days as a purveyor of finely made aprons. Albert and Peter's grandmother Alice opened the atelier's first shop in 1922.

The apron is foundational. "It's the definition of what I always thought design was," Albert told me on a visit to the Paris showroom. Looking forward to the anniversary that this book celebrates, he had made a study of the apron's shape for the Spring/Summer 2022 collection. Akris, he said, "is about clothes and humans. It's not about fashion; it's about construction, about making a woman feel her best. It's as simple as that."

Over the years, of course, he's brought his personal passions to the collections. Attending Akris shows has been an education in art history. One season, it could be Franz Kline, another it could be Kazimir Malevich. Kline's dynamic brushstrokes inspired the graphic quality of Akris's Fall/Winter 2012 collection, and Malevich's intersecting rectangles were a starting point for Spring/Summer 2015; the resulting pieces looked like canvases come to life.

It was for the Fall/Winter 2014 collection, which also marked his tenth anniversary at Paris Fashion Week, that Albert worked with a contemporary, living artist for the first time. The German photo-artist Thomas Ruff, whose work Albert admires, is also a longtime friend. Albert used Ruff's night vision images for a sleek plunge-front evening dress and a knee-length sheath over-embroidered with three-dimensional tiles. For Fall/Winter 2022, he looked to another German artist, Reinhard Voigt, who reduces his landscapes and portraits to grids. "Reinhard once told me that his motive in art is raising the question of how far reduction can go without abandoning beauty," Albert said. "I can relate."

There's that minimalism notion again – but "reduced" is the wrong way to think about what Akris does. Clean shapes are simply the best showcase for the skills of its St. Gallen craftspeople. The small Swiss city was once responsible for 50 % of the world's embroideries. Chez Akris, the three-dimensional tiles of the Thomas Ruff collection just scratch the surface.

Consider Spring/Summer 2016, a collaboration with the Japanese architect Sou Fujimoto which included one dress made from thin strips of cork and another from square slices of Perspex sealed between two layers of organza. Then there was the scintillating silver foil stripe of Spring/Summer 2020, and the phosporizing (read: glow in the dark) fabric of Spring/Summer 2021. Akris keeps its clients in cashmere double-face – "our clothes must be felt," Albert once told me – but he's also pushing the boundaries of fabric technology, looking to the future and the cutting edge of innovation.

Architecture is another obsession. In fact, it was a trapezoidal building by the young Mexican architect Tatiana Bilbao – one of the seventeen pavilions

in the Jinhua Architecture Park in China commissioned by Ai Weiwei – that, in 2010, inspired the first Akris handbag. You'll never see a logo on an accessory here, but there are other identifying markers. The building's shape resembled an A, and so do the fashion house's bags: A for Alice, A for apron, and A, of course, for Akris. But the atelier's use of geometry is more than just a useful coincidence. In the Spring/Summer 2020 collection, Albert inset trapezoidal shapes into the backs of dresses. "It's good for the physiognomy," he told me. Indeed, they did create a graceful fluidity, elongating the silhouettes and lending them special elegance.

Stealth luxury. Clothes that transcend trends. Non-fashion fashion. All that is what Akris stands for, a quiet powerhouse in an industry that celebrates noisy excess. The family-owned house remains apart, not just because nearly 700 kilometers and a mountain range separate Paris from St. Gallen, but also because of its soul. A hundred years ago, Albert's grandmother Alice set out to make women's lives better and more beautiful, and that very much remains Albert's lifework today. "To feel well in the clothes," he has said. "That's the point."

TRAPEZOID, Musée de l'Homme   While researching visual vocabulary for the upcoming Akris accessory line, a trapezoidal pavilion caught my eye. Designed by a young Mexican architect, Tatiana Bilbao, it was one of seventeen pavilions in the Jinhua Architecture Park near Shanghai, China. In a symbolic way, its shape spelled "A" to me. Introduced in this collection, the trapezoid became our logo-less logo, representing the "A" in Akris, tying together the journey of our family house from Alice to Albert to Ai.

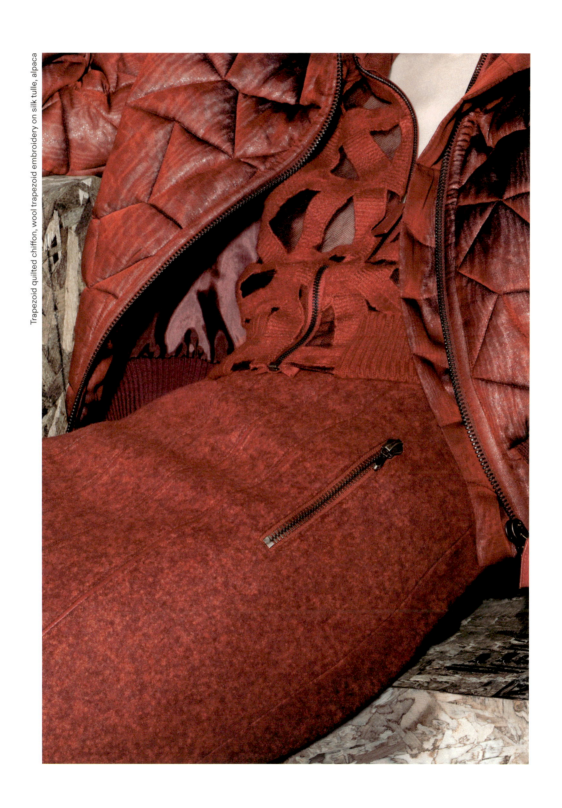

Trapezoid quilted chiffon, wool trapezoid embroidery on silk tulle, alpaca

Wedding Tower print on wool double-face

JOSEPH MARIA OLBRICH'S WEDDING TOWER, Salle Wagram   Pure luxury sportswear, rustic softness, brown and golden suedes were new obsessions, and we flirted with a little edge, adding zipper details to long and lean dresses. The inspiration was a photo of Austrian architect Joseph Maria Olbrich's Wedding Tower on Mathildenhöhe in Darmstadt, Germany, bathed in beautiful fall colors. One of the architect's most beautiful buildings... and the print of the season. We translated his Art Nouveau façades into modern crochet, lace and embroidery. The Salle Wagram, a bohemian dance hall from 1865, provided the perfect backdrop.

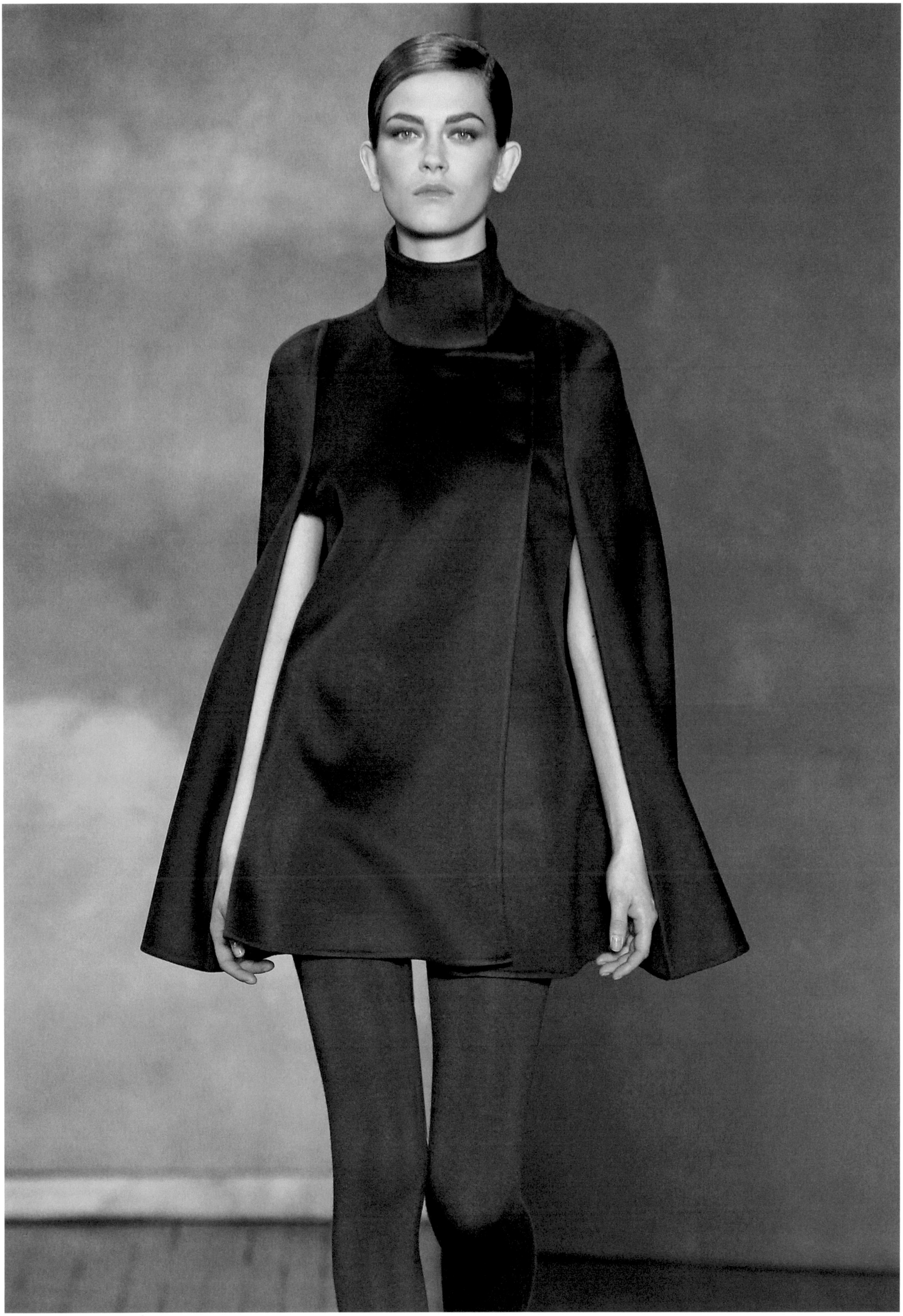

Cashmere double-face

Alpaca/wool double-face, cashmere/silk knit

IT'S ALL ABOUT THE JACKET, Grand Palais   The jacket is the departure of every collection. It represents what Akris is all about. A jacket has its inner life. The pivotal point is the shoulder, from where it floats weightlessly around the body. The drape of the fabric is a factor that cannot be overestimated. For this season we used everything that is the essence of Akris. Cashmere, alpaca, wool, double-face and, most excitingly, cotton silk jersey in the first look. A blazer that wears like a cardigan. A unique experience when worn against the skin. Haptic beauty is essential to me.

Pebblestone St. Gallen embroidery

90 YEARS – 90 LOOKS IN A ROBERTO BURLE MARX GARDEN, Palais de Chaillot   We were celebrating our ninetieth anniversary and we thought about doing something unexpected. My work is often referred to as a minimalism of clear lines, and when we came across a picture of a garden in São Paulo by Brazilian landscape architect Roberto Burle Marx, it inspired me to explore organic lines and soft tailoring. They influenced how the entire collection was cut. The Pebblestone embroidery patchwork dresses were quite seductive and new.

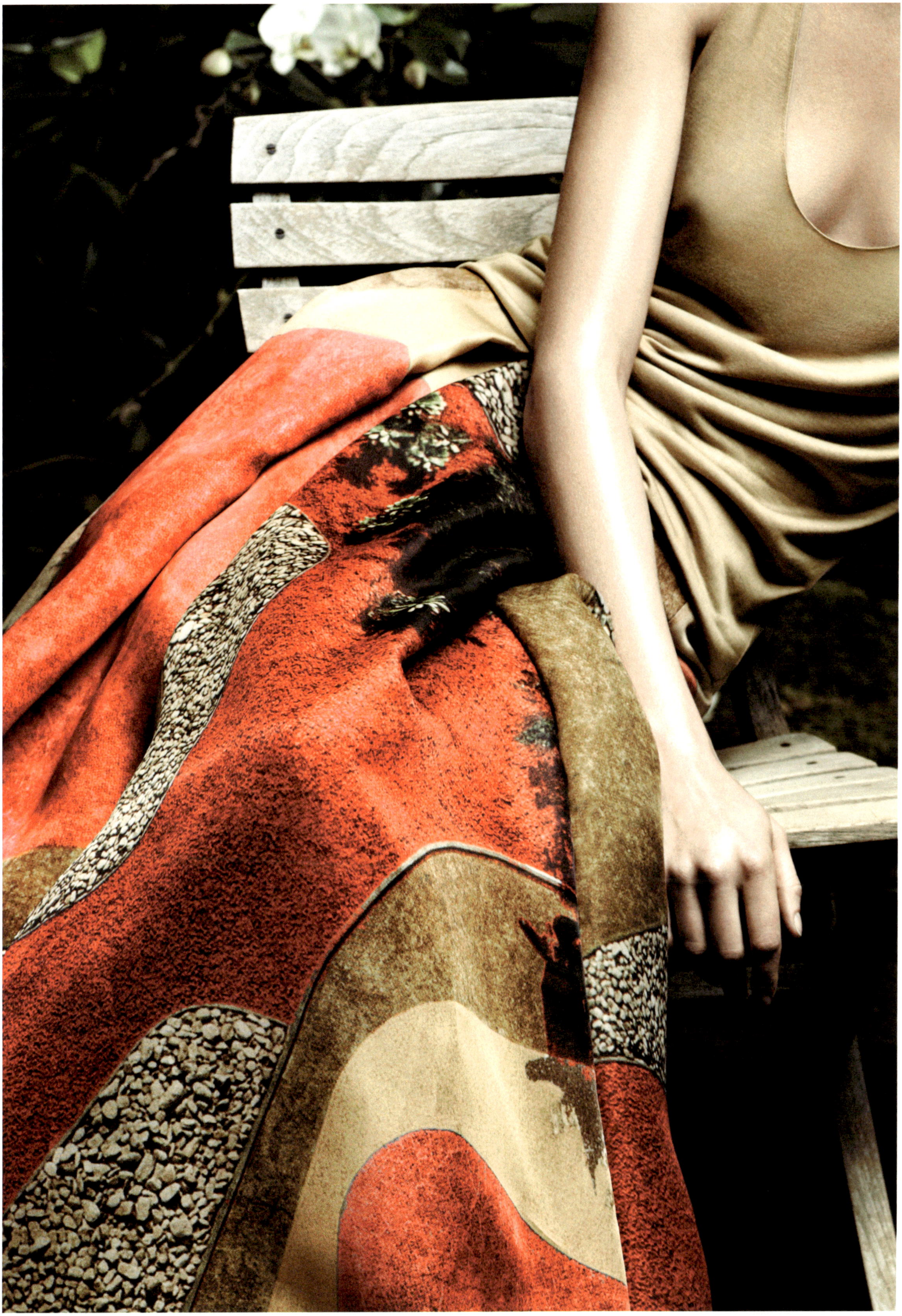

Silk jersey, silk organza

Twisted cotton

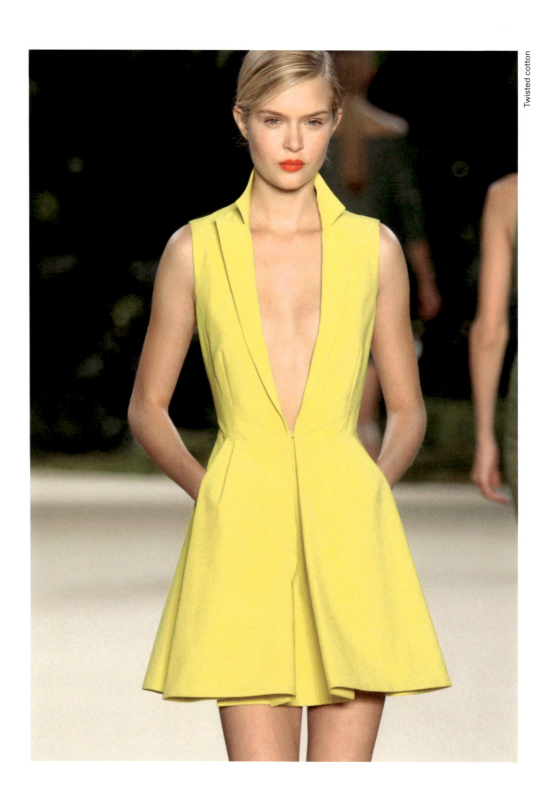

A Woman with a Purpose

Akris's history begins with a woman who knows what she wants: Alice Kriemler-Schoch

By Anne Urbauer

Alice Kriemler-Schoch grew up on her parents' farm as the eighth of eleven children, completed a tailoring apprenticeship and at nineteen joined her aunt's seamstress business, which specialized in aprons. Soon, thanks to her natural air of authority, she took on managerial responsibilities there. After six years, she handed in her notice and, as a newlywed, decided to start her own apron workshop.

She saved up for an entire year to buy her first sewing machine, a black Singer, and set up her first atelier in 1922 at the age of twenty-six.

Her husband, Albert Kriemler, came from Speicher, a village near St. Gallen, now home to Akris's fabric warehouse, pattern-making studio and logistics center. She asked him to help out with the sales side of the business.

A hundred years ago, aprons were ubiquitous: "the hallmark of the working woman," as Jolanda Spirig's book *Schürzennäherinnen* (Apron Seamstresses) about the period puts it. Women who worked outside the home were the young entrepreneur's main target group. Elaborate handcrafted aprons in high-quality fabrics with embroidery, inserts and other decorations were popular with shop-girls serving customers in stores. Alice Kriemler-Schoch's aprons were different: more sober, in keeping with the spirit of the 1920s, made of the best fabrics and with the finest workmanship.

In May 1922, while she was still getting the atelier up and running, her son Max was born, followed a year later by his brother Ernst.

During this period, St. Gallen endured crisis after crisis. The First World War had put an end to the Belle Époque embroidery boom. Many businesses were forced to close.

Alice's young atelier survived the worldwide economic crisis and continued to grow. Soon she employed eight seamstresses and two pattern-makers.

She had an acute sense of fabrics and fit. "Kriemler aprons were the only ones that had rounded darts to reflect the lines of the body. They were elegantly tailored and chic," her grandson Albert Kriemler notes.

Alice had short hair and usually wore plain black pinafore dresses with flat shoes. She was athletic, and loved to ski and to swim at Drei Weieren, a bathing resort above St. Gallen, where a century later her grandson Albert shot a film about his Fall/Winter 2021 collection.

"She had a natural sense of herself as an entrepreneur, on an equal footing with men. That was very unusual in the business culture of that era. Women were not allowed to vote or stand in elections in Switzerland back then," Peter Kriemler comments.

In her leadership role, she insisted on the highest standards of craftsmanship, punctuality and tidiness in the workplace. She was keen to ensure that her female staff could improve their skills, and also stood by them when they had private problems. "She walked the walk of a culture of respect, addressing employees as equals," says Albert Kriemler. "She had a strong personality and was kind," recalled Annarös Leuenberger, who started out as an apprentice seamstress in 1946 and worked at Akris for sixty years.

Alice Kriemler-Schoch in her office

Alice and Albert Kriemler-Schoch with their sons
Max (left) and Ernst, 1930s

Alice in front of her new home, Villa Fels
at Felsenstrasse 38, acquired in 1939

In February 1939, on the eve of the Second World War, Alice bought a disused four-story office building in St. Gallen, along with the neighboring plot of land, including Villa Fels, which gave the street its name. At first, she rented out all but one floor, where her seamstresses worked.

To this day, Felsenstrasse 40 with its brick building is Akris's address and the fount of its creativity. A modern apartment building replaced the old villa in the 1950s.

Alice shared stories about the challenges that arose during the war with other women at the St. Gallen Club of Professional and Business Women (BGF). "It's been interesting. Good to be part of it," she wrote in her diary in May 1943.

In 1944, her husband died suddenly of a heart attack when he was just fifty-nine. Her sons broke off their studies to assist their mother. Max had been preparing for a medical degree, while his brother was doing an apprenticeship as a tailor.

"It was a really difficult situation. My mother had thirty employees and no one to travel around and find new customers as my father had done," Max later recalled. Apparently Max proclaimed at the time that he would take on that role for "a year but not a day longer."

Five years later, at the end of 1949, Alice signed the company over to him. His brother Ernst followed his beloved Rosmarie to St. Moritz and opened a fashion store that is still in operation.

Alice continued to work for the company into her eighties, although aprons were no longer center-stage. Akris's future lay with other garments: dresses, blouses and skirts. In 1952, Max was already turning more of a profit from dresses alone than from aprons.

This meant that Alice had more spare time. She learned English before setting off on a four-month trip to see her sister Ida, who was living in Florida. At sixty-two, she passed her driving test and her first car, a Fiat, was a gift from her sons.

Max was thirty-seven when he introduced his mother to his future wife in 1959. "My mother-in-law gave me a very considerate introduction to the business. She was delighted that I was working in the company and keen to continue learning," Ute Kriemler later commented on her first years as part of the family.

"You must never say you can't do something; just have a go and then suddenly you will find that you can do it," Alice Kriemler-Schoch wrote in the diary she kept until her death in 1972.

Akris atelier building at Felsenstrasse 40, acquired in 1939

Alice and her son Max having tea in Bad Ragaz, Switzerland

Alice passed her driving exam at the age of sixty-two

Fashion Is Always About Moving Forward

A family business: from Max and Ute Kriemler
to Albert and Peter Kriemler

By Anne Urbauer

Max Kriemler never studied management, nor did he
do an apprenticeship as a tailor. He took over his mother's
company in 1949, when he was twenty-seven. He was
quick to make decisions and learned to rely on his intuition.
As a result, he grew more self-confident and had the
courage to do things in his own particular way.

During the thirty-eight years that Max was in
sole charge, his enormous energy raised the fashion
house to a new level. He combined entrepreneurial vision,
dynamism and creativity.

As a seventeen-year-old high-school student,
he had juggled with the letters in his mother's name, taking the first letters of "Alice Kriemler-Schoch" to compose
a modern new company name that sounds good in
any language: Akris. In 1960, he adopted this as the official
designation for the house.

He met his wife Ute Winkhaus, an athletic
young German, while skiing. Albert, their first son, was born
in February 1960, later followed by a sister, Susi, and a
brother, Peter.

Max decided at an early stage where his ambi-
tion lay: Paris, the world capital of fashion. He attended
fashion shows and established contacts. In 1969, he met
French designer Ted Lapidus at a cotton symposium
in St. Gallen. At the time, Lapidus was to French fashion
"[w]hat François Truffaut was to film," to cite *The New York
Times*: the embodiment of the Nouvelle Vague (French
New Wave) and darling of the twenty-somethings. Brigitte
Bardot, Jane Fonda, Alain Delon and the Beatles wore
Lapidus. For almost fifteen years, Akris manufactured the
great innovator's prêt-à-porter collections under license.

As significant as the transfer of know-how
through Lapidus was, Max also admired the sophistication
and classicism of Hubert de Givenchy's fashion. He
wanted Akris to produce the new prêt-à-porter collections
"Givenchy Nouvelle Boutique" and "Givenchy 5" with
Akris, and after a show he contacted de Givenchy's brother,
who was inter alia in charge of production.

Jean-Claude de Givenchy commissioned Akris
to produce the collections and make the preparations
for the associated fashion shows in Paris, as well as invit-
ing and attending to Givenchy's international clients.
The de Givenchy brothers remained family friends. Hubert
de Givenchy adored Ute Kriemler, due to her wit, charm,
warm-heartedness and charisma.

Two companies Max acquired in the early 1970s
would shape the history of Akris well into the next gen-
eration: Walter Stark and Damaco. Walter Stark produced
blouses and dresses in the finest fabrics such as chiffon
or georgette and had a distributor in Japan – the Aoi
company in Kobe. In 1975, Max presented an Akris collection designed specifically for the Japanese market. Aoi
imported and distributed Akris until Akris Japan became
established as an independent entity and subsidiary
in 2002.

Handing responsibility over to the next genera-
tion is a critical moment for any family business. Max
wasted no time on that front either. Shortly after his sixty-
fifth birthday on May 31, 1987, he transferred management
of the fashion house to his young sons. Their sister Susi

Max Kriemler on his way to meet clients, with sample cases of his mother's aprons

Max and Ute Kriemler on the terrace of their new apartment at Felsenstrasse 38, 1960s

Max Kriemler (right), overseeing a fitting in the Akris atelier

became a doctor, taking up what had been Max's dream profession when he was young.

After completing his law degree, Peter introduced computers into the company during his first years there. Ernst Wegmann, who works with the brothers as CFO, actively supported this process. Somewhat later, electronic systems were also incorporated into the design and pattern-making departments.

Ute Kriemler began to play a new role during the transitional phase. She traveled to New York with Albert and played an active part in expanding Akris, both there and then throughout the United States. "She had a special talent for initiating and maintaining relationships," Peter Kriemler notes. In 1988, Bergdorf Goodman ordered the Akris collection for the first time. That marked the start of a close relationship that continues to this day with the legendary department store on Fifth Avenue in New York.

Joe Boitano, probably the most famous general merchandising manager of the day in North America, forged the way as a pioneering purchasing agent. He later commented: "Ute Kriemler was one of the most elegant women I have ever met: refined, smart, intelligent, warm, sincere, graceful, and besides – what a businesswoman! She embodied the Akris collection like no one else."

Joan Kaner, for many years Fashion Director at luxury department store group Neiman Marcus, recalls that she "took a liking to Ute Kriemler from the very first moment." "She was warm, charming, authentic – she had all those positive traits that you certainly don't encounter every day in the fashion world."

The 1990s saw the fashion house truly arriving on the Parisian scene, opening a dedicated showroom and French headquarters on Avenue Pierre 1er de Serbie in the 16th arrondissement, as well as launching its first boutique in the capital and attaining membership of the Fédération Française de la Couture, du Prêt-à-Porter des Couturiers et des Créateurs de Mode (now known as the Fédération de la Haute Couture et de la Mode), the authoritative body that grants access to the official Paris fashion shows. In 2004, Albert Kriemler presented his first official show in Paris.

Peter manages the technical and commercial side of Akris with entrepreneurial flair. Supporting his brother and his team is important to him. "We have an extremely lean structure and clear rules, but we want our team members to be able to decide and be independent, not least the younger ones," he says. He still does the calculations for every piece. "I can turn up anywhere in the company at any time, be it in the fabric warehouse, the production department or the boutique, which means I'm familiar with all the designs and can talk to any employee about a product. I take a look and ask questions, but also provide information. My good memory is a great help in that respect."

In 2009, Albert established the trapezoid as an unofficial hallmark of his signature style, which otherwise deliberately eschews visible branding or logomania. It represents the contour of the apron that marked the inception of the Akris story, the A-line cut that plays a central role in Albert Kriemler's work and references

Peter Kriemler in the Akris showroom in St. Gallen

Jim Gold (CEO Bergdorf Goodman), Ute Kriemler and
Burt Tansky (CEO Neiman Marcus), late 2000s

Iconic trapezoidal clasp of an Ai bag

proportions of the golden ratio, one of the cornerstones in his creative vision.

Just prior to this, in 2008, in the middle of the largest financial crisis since 1929, the brothers had taken over a German bag manufacturer. It specialized in processing the finest horsehair. Full of enthusiasm for this textile material, Albert began developing his first handbag, a tote known as the Ai bag.

Once again, Akris emerged from a global crisis much stronger. As it had earlier, by taking over a company with first-class designers, tailors and pattern-makers, and expertise in working with a rarefied material, the house had seized the opportunity to add an important category to the Akris collection: accessories.

Today, much of the Akris collection is manu-factured in Romania, where Peter, together with technical director Wolf-Dieter Lang, set up a state-of-the-art in-house production facility called Artifex in 2005. Employees receive initial and further training in Switzerland and are in touch with the parent company in St. Gallen every day.

After the European Union's eastward expansion in 2005, Romania was no longer a "third country" but an EU Member State. "In contrast to the approach adopted by many fashion companies in France and Italy, we were convinced that we wanted to stick to our own manufactur-ing structures. Akris's understated minimalist fashion and the range of delicate fabrics call for outstanding production expertise. The company's fully vertical structure has proved its worth for Akris for over a hundred years," Peter Kriemler explains.

Evening gowns and double-face coats and jackets are largely hand-sewn in the ateliers in Mendrisio, in the Swiss canton of Ticino, and carefully pressed into shape thanks to know-how from the men's tailoring department. Peter built up this production in the boom years of the 1990s, in keeping with the house's principles.

Architecture, an inspiration and ideal in Albert's oeuvre, is also a deep-rooted thematic strand that runs through Peter's work throughout his career. Reflecting the entrepreneurs' principles, the production facilities are characterized by limpid clarity, top-quality materials with nuanced finishes and good lighting. You gain a real sense of the space and the people. The brothers were meticulous in supervising construction of their twenty boutiques and numerous stores-in-stores, initially with Ticino-based architect Ferruccio Robbiani and subsequently for many years in collaboration with Christoph Sattler and Rita Ahlers from Munich. The sensuous minimalism of the most recent projects in Tokyo and Washington was devised and implemented with David Chipperfield Architects.

After many years during which Peter traveled and managed overseas markets himself, in 2018 Melissa Beste was appointed Global CEO, with responsibility for these markets and sales. Melissa is based in New York. Previously, she headed Akris's subsidiary in the key U.S. market. As well as managing the head office, Peter over-sees the overall management, while Albert continues to hold responsibility for creating all the collections and for the corporate image. Important decisions are always taken jointly.

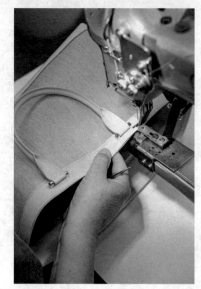

Crafting an Ai bag in the atelier in
Obertshausen, Germany

Akris manufacturing site Artifex in Focșani, Romania

Sewing double-face garments by hand in the atelier in
Mendrisio, Switzerland

As changing shopping habits, particularly among younger customers, have increasingly seen purchases shifting to the Internet, Peter Kriemler set up a new e-commerce store – just in time before the COVID-19 pandemic emerged in 2020, forcing lengthy lockdowns worldwide.

For Albert, this caesura provided an occasion to dedicate the collections he could not show in Paris to his hometown of St. Gallen and its almost one thousand years of textile expertise, as the place where he and Peter have been steering an independent path in fashion together for thirty-five years, respecting skills honed over three generations.

Not all family businesses manage to strengthen the spirit of cooperation over generations and ensure constant renewal so that the firm continues to thrive. How did this culture emerge, and how is it transmitted in the family?

Since their first day together at the fashion house, Albert and Peter Kriemler have met with Ernst Wegmann every morning for half an hour to an hour, in order to catch up, ask questions and see how the others respond to particular ideas. "It's been an unusually informal process and has come about organically as we worked together," Peter Kriemler underlines. "We didn't draw up a set of rules." After working closely together for so many years, they can sense each other's reactions and understand one another almost without words. Their relationship has matured over a long period, with untrammeled mutual trust. All decisions about the company's business are made like this; there is neither an agenda nor minutes.

At the same time, the brothers are sustained by principles established by the two generations before them. Show respect. Be courageous. Do what you think is right, even if the world is not yet convinced. Cultivate curiosity about the next steps. "For us, it's not about what we've achieved, it's keeping moving. We're always asking 'What's next?'" says Albert Kriemler. "Because fashion is always about moving forward, and for us fashion means a perpetual process of evolving that will probably never come to a halt."

Akris boutique on Old Bond Street
in London, sketch by architect
Christoph Sattler

Akris boutique in Washington D.C., designed by
David Chipperfield Architects

Peter and Albert Kriemler backstage in Paris

A Century in Fashion

1922	Alice Kriemler-Schoch sets up her atelier for apron-making
1935	First order from Globus department store, Zurich
1939	Alice and her husband Albert buy the building at Felsenstrasse 40, today the seat of the house
1944	Max joins the company at the age of twenty-two, following the passing of his father
1949	Max takes over responsibilities for the atelier from his mother
1953	First showroom in Zurich opens with a collection of blouses, skirts and dresses, spurring department stores Robert Ober, Feldpausch and Jelmoli into carrying the Akris collection
1956	Akris employs 150 staff members
1960	Akris, an acronym composed of letters from Alice Kriemler-Schoch's name – **A, Kri** and **S** – is registered as the official name of the house
1969	Max Kriemler meets French designer Ted Lapidus and starts a collaboration to manufacture ready-to-wear collections for the Parisian house
1970	Max acquires Walter Stark, a distinguished blouse manufacturer in St. Gallen
1972	Akris stops making aprons
1973	Max Kriemler acquires Damaco Zurich, an atelier for superior suits and coats made of double-face and other high-end fabrics
1975	With Aoi as distributor, Max offers his first Akris collection for the Japanese market
1978	Max establishes fabric company Cosilan for fine cotton and silk
	Akris starts making blouses for Swiss Air flight attendants
	Max creates the "Alpha" coat, made of finest cashmere double-face
1979	Albert Kriemler joins the house after graduating from high school, subsequently taking over all creative responsibilities
	Hubert de Givenchy officially appoints Akris to manufacture and distribute his "Givenchy 5" and "Givenchy Nouvelle Boutique" ready-to-wear collections

1985	Swiss graphic designer Georg Staehelin develops the Akris logo with Albert Kriemler
1987	Peter Kriemler joins the company. The management of the family business is officially handed over to the third generation, Albert and Peter Kriemler
1988	Dawn Mello, at that time fashion director of Bergdorf Goodman, places the first order of an Akris collection for the renowned department store on New York's Fifth Avenue
1989	Max Kriemler acquires the apartment in the 16th arrondissement which will become the future Akris showroom in Paris
1995	First global advertising campaign with photographer Steven Klein and model Stella Tennant
	First Akris boutique in Paris on Rue du Faubourg Saint-Honoré
1996	Launch of the Designer Sportswear Collection Akris punto
	Akris becomes a member of what is now the Fédération de la Haute Couture et de la Mode in Paris
Mid-1990s	Expansion into department stores in the USA and Canada with partners Neiman Marcus, Saks Fifth Avenue and Holt Renfrew
1997	Opening of first boutique in the USA in Boston, first boutique in Monte Carlo in Monaco, and first store-in-store at Bergdorf Goodman in New York
1999	Akris Korea Co. Ltd is founded with Ms Eun Jung Choi and headquarters in Seoul
2002	Akris Japan K. K. is founded with new headquarters in Tokyo
2003	Opening of a new production facility in Mendrisio, Switzerland
2004	First official press défilé in Paris at the Akris showroom in Avenue Pierre Ier de Serbie
2005	Artifex, the new production site in Romania, is inaugurated
	First collaboration of Albert Kriemler with choreographer John Neumeier for the 2006 Vienna Philharmonic New Year's concert
2006	"Akris: Fashions from St. Gallen" in St. Gallen's Textile Museum is featured as a part of a series of exhibitions on art and apparel

2008	Albert Kriemler is awarded the Swiss Grand Award for Design by the Swiss Federal Office of Culture
	Albert Kriemler's collection is inspired by an artist who was also a personal friend, Ian Hamilton Finlay. Images of Finlay's garden in Little Sparta, Scotland, launch innovative digital prints
2009	With the Fall/Winter 2009 collection, Albert introduces the trapezoid as the symbol for Akris
	For Spring/Summer 2010, Akris launches its first collection of handbags and accessories with the trapezoidal Ai bag and rarefied horsehair as its signature material
	The Merit Award, Switzerland's most prestigious design award, is bestowed on Albert Kriemler
2010	Albert receives the Star Award from Fashion Group International (FGI) in New York
2014	For Fall/Winter 2014, Albert creates a collection with German artist Thomas Ruff, who attends the défilé in Paris. This marks the house's first collaboration with a living artist
2016	The magazine *Wallpaper** bestows its "Design Award 2016 Best Alliance" for the collaboration with Tokyo-based architect Sou Fujimoto on Albert Kriemler's Spring/Summer 2016 collection
	The Couture Council of The Museum at FIT bestows its 2016 Award for Artistry of Fashion on Albert Kriemler. For the first time, Albert shows a collection, Spring/Summer 2017, during New York Fashion Week. He collaborates with Cuban-American artist, Carmen Herrera
2019	Peter Kriemler launches a new e-commerce site for Akris and Akris punto
2020–2022	Due to the the temporary suspension of Paris Fashion Week, Albert Kriemler unveils his Spring/Summer 2021 collection, a collaboration with German artist Imi Knoebel, in an exclusive film directed by Anton Corbijn. Akris stages three subsequent collection films in St. Gallen, dedicating these collections to the deep relationship between the house and its home city
2022	Two new Akris boutiques are opened, making them the first with a new design concept by architect David Chipperfield. The boutique in Washington, D.C. opens on May 8, Ute Kriemler's 85th birthday; the new store in Tokyo opens on May 31, Max Kriemler's 100th birthday
October 1, 2022	Akris celebrates a century in fashion

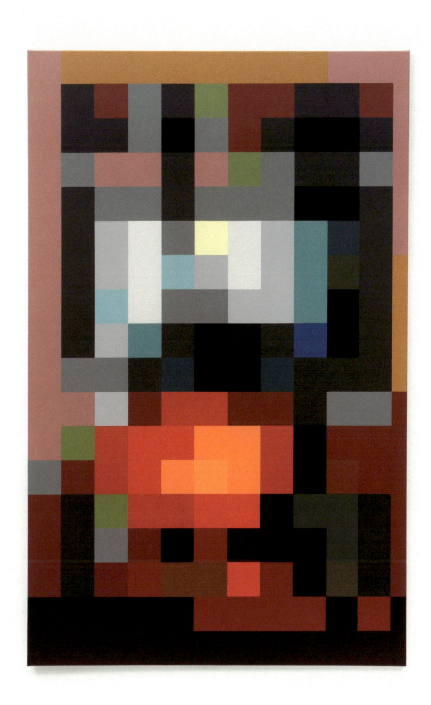

ALBERT KRIEMLER × REINHARD VOIGT, SQUARE, University of St. Gallen   The work of German artist Reinhard Voigt, whose 1960s colored square paintings read as digital pixels to our modern gaze, sparked a collection built on squares. We sewed together two squares of fabric for an asymmetrical fall of a dress as a pattern-making play. Created in our lightest neoprene and wool, it had this "wow"-worthy effect. Serendipity devised the opportunity to stage it in the newly finished St. Gallen university building named SQUARE by Japanese architect and friend Sou Fujimoto, constructed out of modular squares.

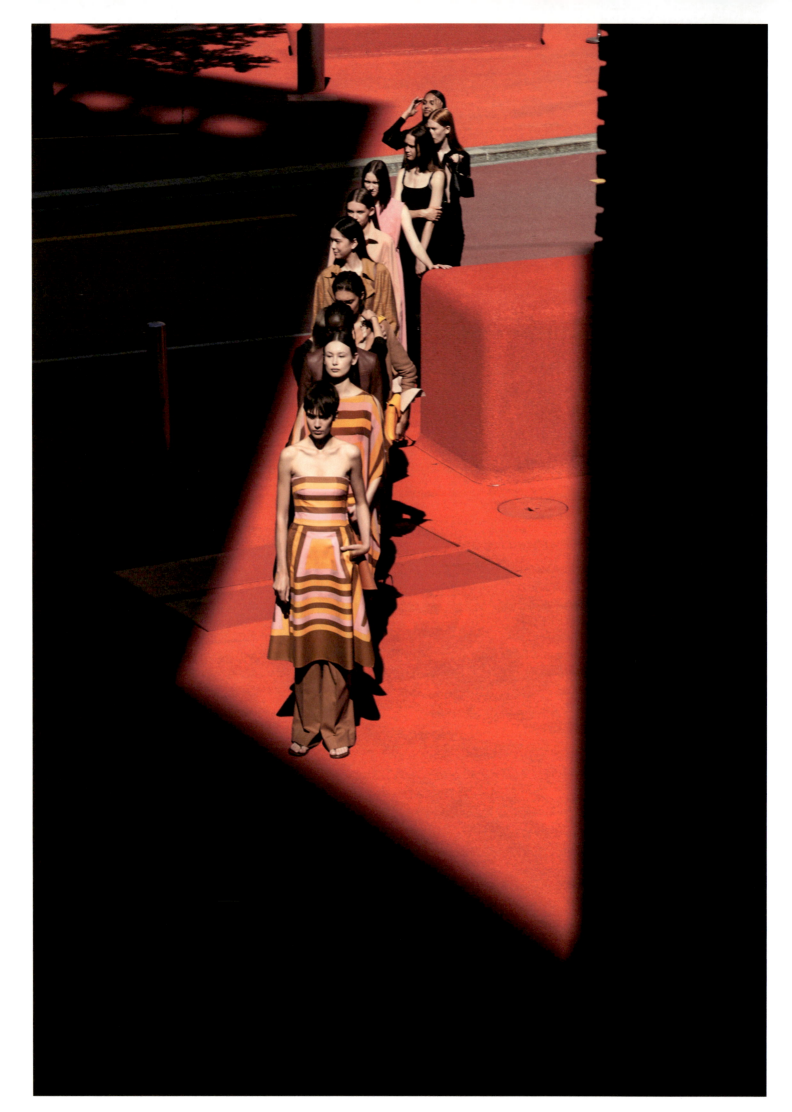

Silk lurex organza, silk rib knit, silk piqué knit

A WOMAN AND AN APRON, Roter Platz, St. Gallen   It is all about an essence. My grandmother Alice constructed Akris sewing aprons from St. Gallen fabrics and embroideries. The image of her donning her apron after breakfast to go to the atelier every day signified to me a confidence and readiness to step out into the world. I immediately thought of a modern take on the suit. The combination of apron skirts or dresses over pants. Modern, versatile, playful.

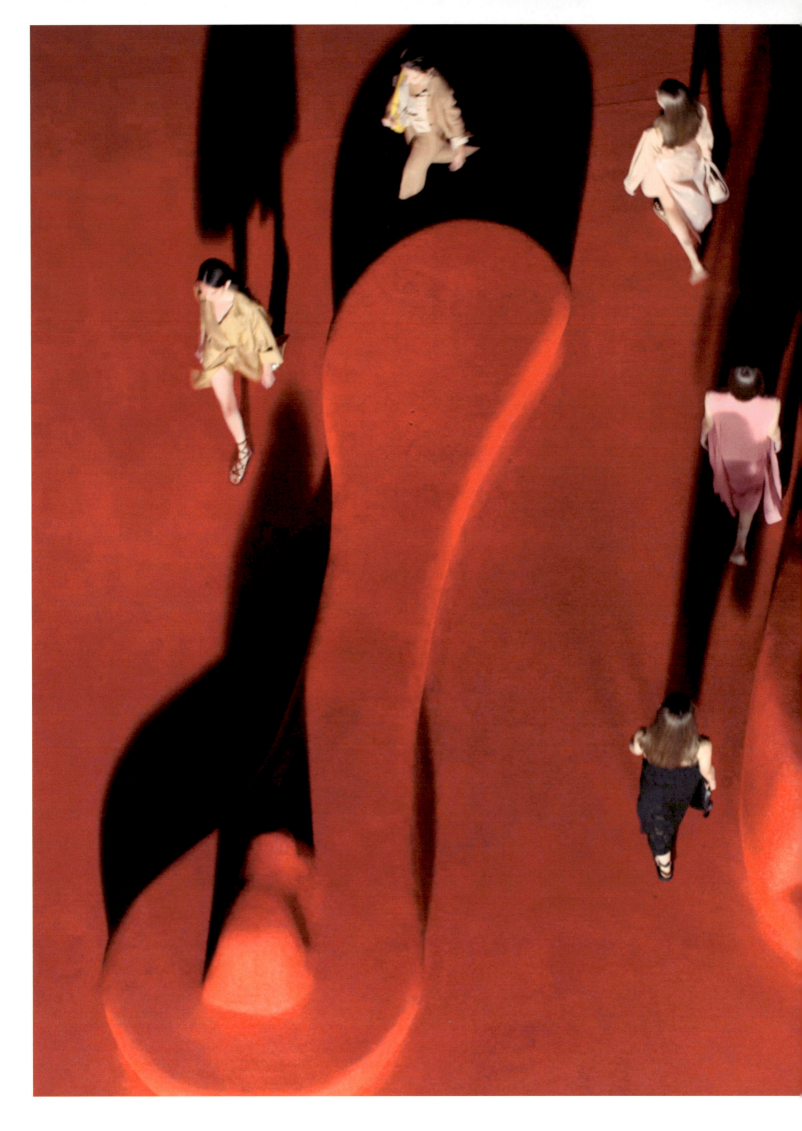

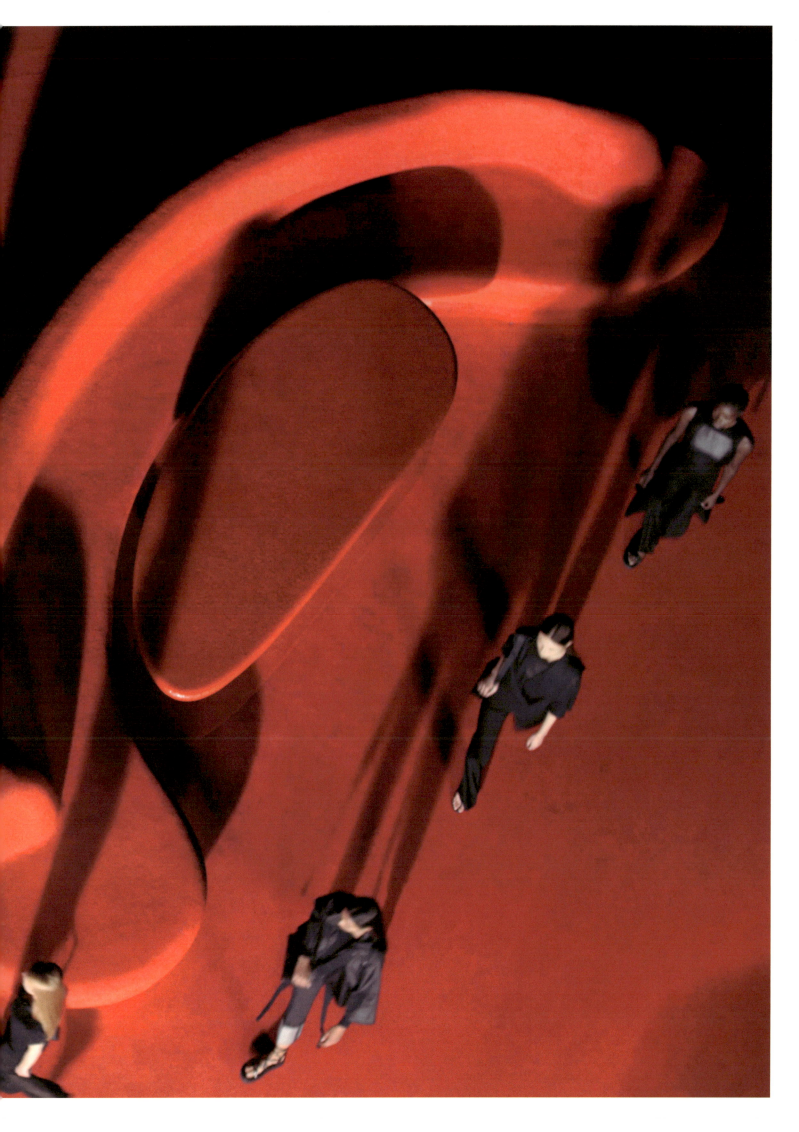

Stripe cotton double-face | Linen/wool crêpe double-face, cotton/silk rib knit

Silk/cotton rib knit, linen/wool crêpe double-face

St. Gallen Map print on neoprene, wool stripes embroidery on tulle

A WOMAN ON A WALK, Abbey Library, St. Gallen   Walking is an act of freedom, and often it is used as a version of escape. Effortlessness and movement were very important to me in this year of lockdown: the idea of a woman putting on a layered, enveloping cover to walk through the streets, nature, parks of her town. Staged at St. Gallen's Abbey library and at Drei Weieren lakes, the collection is an homage to the home and heart of Akris. I wanted to play with everything that is at the core of our house. Most visible in the St. Gallen Map print, revealing the location of the Akris atelier on a second glance.

Cashmere double-face, Infinite and Second Glance St. Gallen embroidery

The St. Gallen Story

How can a designer in a small town in Switzerland create fashion for discerning women all around the globe? That's a question Albert Kriemler often hears in interviews. An attempt to explain this enigma

By Anne Urbauer

If you were asked to think of one place where fabric and fashion have truly deep roots, St. Gallen, the city of embroidery, would spring to mind. The origins of this cluster of excellence in textiles can be traced back to linen woven by monks in the Middle Ages. The earliest extant documentation of this practice is held in the Abbey Library at the Benedictine Abbey of St. Gall, established in 747 and named after the itinerant Irish monk Gallus. The monastery library, one of the most sumptuous and beautiful in the world, is now a UNESCO World Heritage Site. Linen made the city prosperous. St. Gallen's chamber of commerce, founded in 1466, is probably the oldest in the Western world.

In the eighteenth century the mechanization of textile manufactories turned eastern Switzerland into an industrial stronghold. When low-cost British cotton began to penetrate the market, Swiss manufacturers shifted their focus to high-quality, industrially produced embroidery. From the late nineteenth century on, elegant ladies would stroll along promenades around the world in elaborately embroidered dresses and adorn their homes with St. Gallen embroidery. Painter Emil Nolde taught budding pattern-makers at the technical drawing school of the Museum of Industry and Trade, founded in 1878; Swiss artist Sophie Taeuber-Arp also studied there. It became the St. Gallen Textile Museum in 1982, with collections that now comprise over 65,000 objects.

In 1910, embroidery was the most important industry in Switzerland and St. Gallen attracted entrepreneurs from all over the world, especially from the U.S. In 1914, one in three St. Gallen residents came from abroad. A university was founded and has now become one of the top international business schools. Manufacturers, merchants, embroiderers, dyers and finishers offering or seeking goods, services and information would meet in the imposing Textile Exchange. Switzerland's economic strength was grounded in the innovative energy of the textile industry; its global trade relations established the traditionally international perspective that has shaped this small landlocked country for centuries.

The First World War and the global economic crisis in the 1930s ended this boom. Nine out of ten jobs in the textile sector disappeared. The industry recovered after 1945. Nowadays St. Gallen embroidery once again numbers among the most significant and innovative materials in haute couture. And that's not the only sector where it makes its mark: embroidery techniques are increasingly deployed in high-tech and IT products. History is a good thing; the future is even better.

Many spots in the city recall this glorious textile heritage, such as the heritage-listed "Tröckneturm" (Drying Tower), where lengths of fabric used to be dried after dyeing, while the term *Bleiche* in various placenames reveals that fabrics were once bleached in these areas.

In 2005 Swiss artist Pipilotti Rist and architect Carlos Martinez transformed one of these parts of town, the "Bleicheli," into a futuristic urban sculpture swathed in red rubber flooring: a public lounge for everyone, with lights that evoked clouds.

Following pages: Scenes from the St. Gallen embroidery boom
Textile Exchange at Multertor
Main railway station, 1911
Aerial view of St. Gallen by Swiss aviation pioneer
Walter Mittelholzer, 1919
A plunge into the women's pond at "Drei Weieren,"
one of Alice Kriemler-Schoch's favorite spots

St. Gallen photo essay by Iwan Baan

Selbstverständlich: The Akris Spirit

By Daniel Binswanger

Some dresses defy time, such as those that often appear in the rapidly changing cycle of Akris collections. They are of a timelessness that embraces the spirit of the moment. Clothes the likes of which have never been seen before. Moments of futuristic audacity and classic sophistication. Akris moments.

Over the past few decades, Akris has transformed from a medium-sized clothing atelier in St. Gallen into a major international prêt-à-porter fashion house. As a member of the Fédération de la Haute Couture et de la Mode, Akris presents its collections in Paris, the world's fashion capital. This development has progressed with a discretion that is even more astonishing than its rapid pace – no brash image campaigns, no publicity-seeking provocations on the runway, no hasty changes of designer. Many big brands now consist largely of a public relations division, with most of their revenue acquired from accessories. Not so at Akris, where business is still uncompromisingly dedicated to couture.

"Ultimately, only our clothes can communicate what our house actually signifies," says Albert Kriemler. He speaks softly but firmly. However, as soon as issues crucial to his profession are addressed – the collections, the fabrics, his employees – he becomes passionate and resolute. Together with his brother Peter, he has created an astounding St. Gallen design miracle, driven by a permanent quest for innovation that has broadened the savoir-faire of this long-established textile manufacturer in Eastern Switzerland. Albert has reconciled unique top-quality tailoring with an uncompromising, cutting-edge aesthetic.

Time and again, seemingly disparate materials, such as tulle and sequined fabrics, join forces. Time and again, a calculated tension informs the contrast between rigorous, geometric structures and the flow of precious materials. At his shows, Albert Kriemler consistently presents only designs that can actually be worn. Designs that make a confident fashion statement. Designs practically every woman would choose for her wardrobe.

Albert invests his creativity and skill in fashion that feels *selbstverständlich,* an adjective he also uses in English because, as he says, "there is no equivalent for it in English and it is the best way to convey the aesthetic ideal of natural self-evidence that I want to achieve." The result is clothing of effortlessly compelling modernity that defines a woman's presence and comes across in her body-language.

All Kriemler designs are created in a similar fashion. The fabric is the source and impetus of his ideas. It is as if he were starting from scratch every time he comes up with a new design for each garment. Key to the process of creation is the feel and quality of a fabric when he touches it, holds it or drapes it to see how it falls.

Albert is a fabric aficionado. When he goes to textile fairs, he switches off his mobile phone and focuses exclusively on his ceaseless quest for interesting materials with which to experiment. There seems to be no clear boundary between the material from which Kriemler makes the garments and the design he creates for them. It is the fabric that brings the quality of the cut to life. It is the

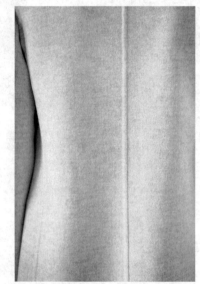

Detail of a wool double-face jacket

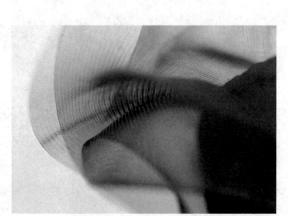

Tulle ribbon detail from the Thomas Ruff collection

wearer who brings the garment to life. Albert and his team carve a new path every time they transform the finest fabric into the perfect silhouette.

Akris is not content with giving high-quality textiles a contemporary touch. It is in the search for the materials itself that cutting-edge design emerges. Expert tailoring of textiles is not just a prerequisite for high quality; it is the space in which Albert's sensitivity unfolds. Herein lies the secret of Akris's elegant sensuality. The quest for style is woven into every product.

"Nowadays, vertical integration is the only way," says Peter Kriemler. Material and workmanship are so important that every step of the process is carried out in-house or entrusted to reliable partners. Akris develops many fabrics itself and often has them produced by Italian or St. Gallen textile firms with which the company has a longstanding collaboration. The garments are produced exclusively in the company's own ateliers; outsourcing the work is not an option because the requisite skills are so exacting.

This applies especially to the double-face technique, the most challenging discipline of couture and the hallmark of Akris. The technique ensures a subtle finish, based on meticulous and demanding work by hand. When Albert Kriemler began designing for Akris in the early 1980s, the house had only three double-face fabrics. The range has been growing continuously since then and now includes double-face production of featherlight fabrics in cotton, silk and linen. The separating devices that this process requires were first developed in-house by a pattern-maker. Cutting machines that can separate such fine fabrics exist today only because Albert discovered the new design potential of these novel textiles – technical innovation translated directly into an aesthetic statement.

No wonder that Akris has become a driving force behind the revival of the textile industry in St. Gallen, the only place in the world that is still home to makers of top-quality embroidery such as Forster Rohner, Bischoff and Jakob Schlaepfer. Akris works regularly with these producers to develop new fabrics that have nothing to do with the retro charm of fleeting fashions but are instead more geometric and utterly state-of-the-art.

Decentralized Urbanity

The exceptional status of Akris is also a consequence of its deep roots in eastern Switzerland. To this day, the company is headquartered in St. Gallen. Albert Kriemler and his teams attend the two annual shows in Paris, while he and his brother Peter maintain customer and business contacts between New York, London and Seoul. However, Albert still comes "home" to the attic in the original main building to design the ten annual collections. How does a designer so far away from metropolitan centers succeed in grasping the subtlest swings of fashion consciousness with such precision? How can he strike a chord season after season with customers scattered across the globe?

"The issue is no longer information," he notes. "Nowadays everyone can easily access enough information to understand which way trends are moving. The

Peter Kriemler in the Paris showroom

Crafting a double-face seam

St. Gallen embroidery

challenge is of an entirely different order: having the courage to be yourself, presenting clothes that have an inimitable signature."

Akris stands for a business model of decentralized urbanity. Being based in allegedly provincial St. Gallen has proved advantageous. Akris benefits from local manufacturing. Maintaining links with the whole world from Eastern Switzerland is also becoming much easier.

During the acute phase of the COVID-19 pandemic, Akris, like other fashion labels, participated in the Paris fashion shows virtually, with videos created in St. Gallen.

It's only when you visit Albert at the Akris headquarters that the magical chemistry between deep local roots and an international spirit begins to make sense. The luxury brand's home base is still in an inconspicuous commercial building on Felsenstrasse in St. Gallen. Albert designs on the top floor, which offers a vista across the city center. The attic is a small-scale biotope of highly concentrated creativity.

Present, Discard, Modify, Present

Pictures of motifs, icons and design quotes are dotted around the walls to revisit and build on. Vintage dresses hang on stands, old Akris models, material that could serve as inspiration. Sketches of the new collection are spread across an entire wall, all with fabric samples to hone the color palette and test the texture of the material: the all-important feel. As in haute couture, Albert works only on real models. He fine-tunes each piece with his pattern-makers, has them present their work, discards it, modifies it, has them present it again, discards it again.

There is another subject that Kriemler talks about with the same intensity and obsessive attention to detail that he applies to the silk jerseys in a new collection or the double-face processing of a particularly elegant jacket: his team members. All design springs from sensory contact with the material, but the creation of value can only succeed when the savoir-faire of a production team is in harmony as well.

"I can't do anything without first-class pattern-makers, who are essential to the process from initial pattern to finished product." He has spent decades building a team that he can work with and that knows how to work with him. Those who make the patterns and models have a profound grasp of the essence of his style. It is not easy, he says, to find someone who can translate his sketches into models of the quality he envisions. Unassuming as always, Albert talks about the people who work closely with him as if they were the indispensable stars of his company. His human resource management is equally unconventional. He encourages his good pattern-makers to do only what they like doing best – and therefore gets the best results.

Albert has developed a distinctive idiom of his own, but he does not consider himself an artist. "Works of art only exist in their own right," he says, but "a dress serves a specific purpose. It is there to be worn by someone." He prefers to compare his work to that of an architect.

Albert Kriemler in his atelier

Denise Burger (right), head and soul of the Paris showroom, overseeing a fitting before the show.

Albert Kriemler working on the Carmen Herrera collection in New York

The art of building also thrives on the creativity of its great masters, yet buildings are not autonomous works of art either. The self-evident sensuality of Akris clothes is indebted to a belief in their functionality. "Wearing a good garment is a bit like living in it."

The designer takes inspiration from both architecture and his love of contemporary art. It is no coincidence that artist collaborations have become an Albert Kriemler trademark. A commitment to the artistic avant-garde plays a perfectly natural role in his understanding of trailblazing fashion.

Unpretentious and inimitably *selbstverständlich*, he walks the fine line between trends and his own approach to form, between experimentation and tradition. Constant renewal is crucial to creating this kind of timeless fashion.

Cotton/silk double-face

MOVEMENT & A TOUCH OF THE 1920s, Salle Delorme, Le Carrousel du Louvre   Aerodynamics, speed, energy – the clean, architectural lines of a super-modern yacht made us think of a streamlined wardrobe. But there is also a touch of the 1920s with luxurious nonchalant sports clothes. Twenties fashion is often remembered for its glitz, but we wanted to underline its move towards simplicity in dressing, and a rejection of formality and multiple layers, in favor of comfort and airiness.

Cotton/silk double-face

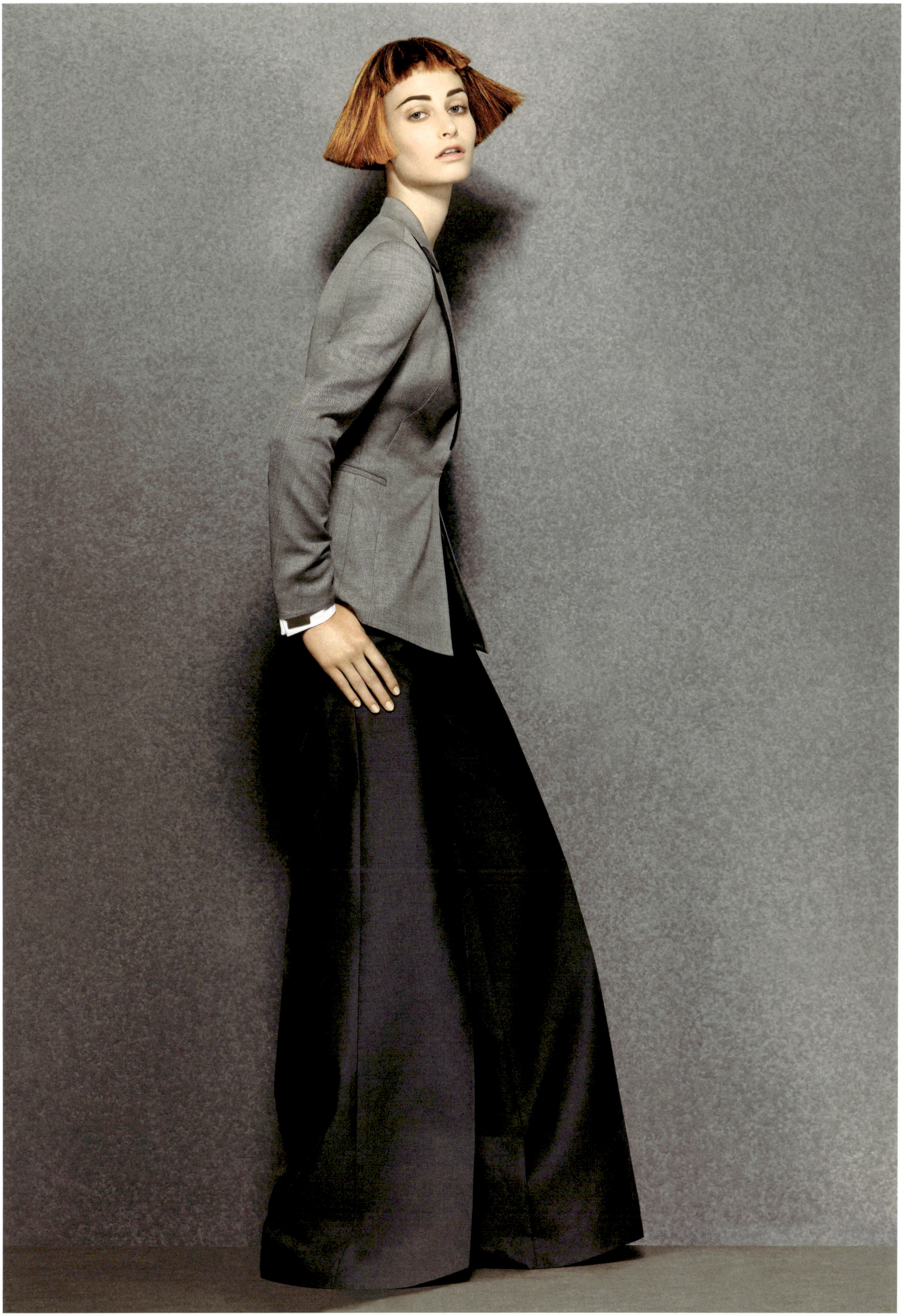

FRANZ KLINE AND THE ABSTRACT EXPRESSIONISTS OF THE 1950s, Palais de Chaillot   A suggestion of space, structure, action, and always an association with architecture. That's Franz Kline for me. I loved how the vertical was more important to him than the horizontal. His *Painting No. 7* was my starting point, as it evokes the pace of modern city life. Our collection was about a woman with purpose and how she can feel relaxed in every moment. And I wanted to do a cool, modern dress out of vertical knitwear in cashmere and silk, very sensuous, very seductive.

Cashmere double-face

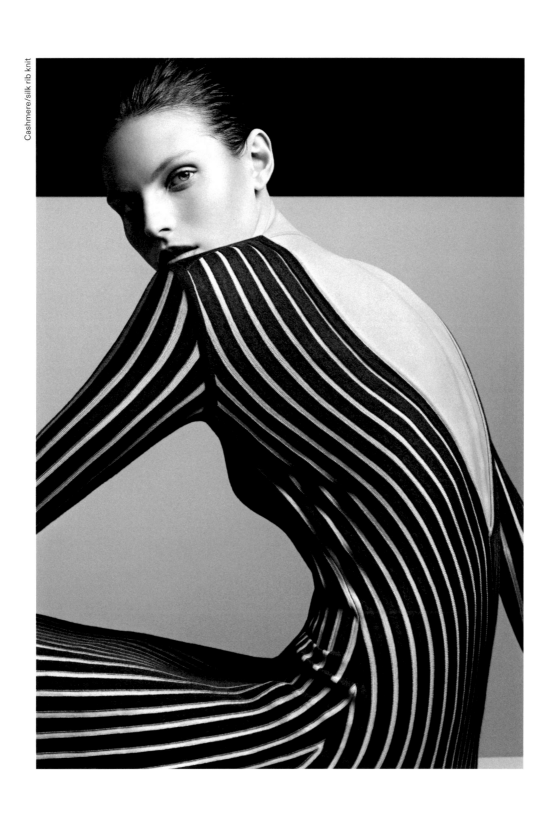

ARCHITECTURE IS ELEMENTAL, Salle Delorme, Le Carrousel du Louvre   Swiss architects Herzog & de Meuron provided endless inspiration for the fabrics of this season. I have been friends with Jacques and Pierre for years and have always admired their interest in the façade of a house. Is it one-, two- or three-layered? What can be done with these layers? The creation of the surface also interests me – as seen in the coat made of aluminum encased in silk georgette imbued with the architects' silvery high-tech "skin" developed for the Walker Art Center in Minneapolis. We added stainless-steel belts handcrafted and finished in St. Gallen. And the interesting surfaces turned them into a highlight of the show. I consider this one of my most distinct fabric-exploration collections.

Aluminum encased in silk georgette

Silk organza over alpaca and silk georgette, wool knit

Parachute silk, cotton/silk double-face

A VISIT TO JAPAN AND THE KYOTO GARDENS, Palais de Chaillot   Returning from a trip to Japan made me think of different kinds of clothes for summer. More relaxed refinement, more simplicity and more ease. The starting point was a relaxed white shirt. Pure perfection. I wanted it to be soft, roomy and light. We used the finest, crispest cotton we could find and riffed on the idea in shantung silk and Sea Island denim, which feels like cashmere for summer.

Soft lamb nappa leather, silk mesh, cotton/silk double-face

Cotton/silk double-face

A Visit to Japan and the Kyoto Gardens

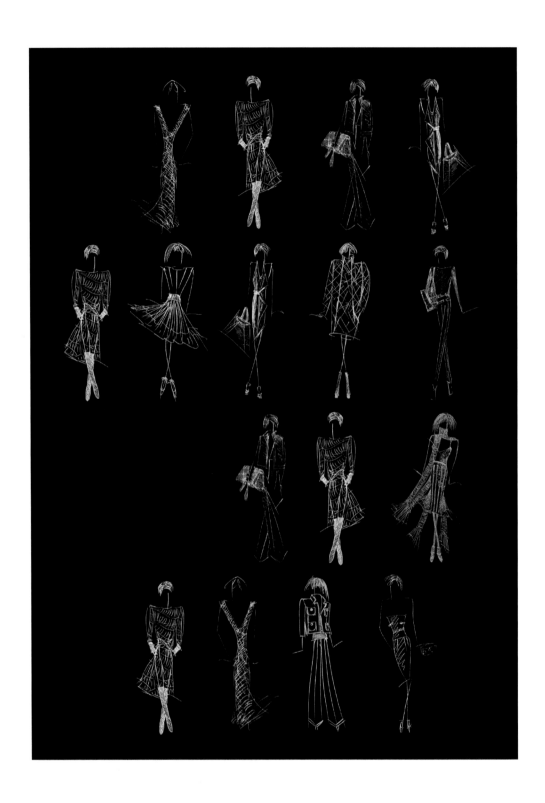

100 YEARS, Palais de Tokyo & Musée d'Art Moderne   It began with the vintage pieces from our archive for the shooting in this book. Most of my team saw those looks I had created between the late 1970s and the 1990s for the first time. They still had this stunning, surprisingly modern effect. We started to work with them and, with the cut of a shoulder, the drape of a skirt, translated them into tokens of today. My team surprised me with the Croquis, a print they had prepared with my sketches from back then. It is witty and charming and it tells a very personal story.

More Than Meets the Eye

They stand independent from each other. But they are designed with a strong sense of interdependence. On the symbiosis of fabric and color

By Jessica Iredale

Sensual minimalism is how Albert Kriemler defines the aesthetic he's cultivated at Akris. Two senses he engages most sublimely are touch and sight. Were one to run through a rack of cashmere coats, the dense velvet hand of Akris's double-face would set it apart from the rest. "Nothing goes into the collection that doesn't feel good," said Albert. Likewise with color and print, rendered with a painterly intensity that appears divined from nature's most saturated and exquisite hues, like the verdant shade of green that distinguishes St. Gallen's Swiss hillsides.

Akris's fabrics and color are definitive qualities that stand independent of each other but are also designed with synergistic radiance. The trained hand can pick out an Akris wool or silk by its tactile flush, just as the trained eye can identify an Akris print by its prismatic palette. But it's the marriage of the two – a fabric chosen because it takes the dye in just the right way – that creates the magic. "It's part of the game to play with fabric," said Albert. "The idea is always to get to the next level."

Albert began experiencing the touch of fine fabrics at a young age, learning the rules and players early on. He spent his childhood ticketing swatches in Akris's studios, where the fabric library dates back to the 1930s. The house's collection of fabrics, from the delicate yet sturdy laces of Alice Kriemler-Schoch's aprons to the techno neoprene used in the Fall/Winter 2022 collection, are meticulously filed and catalogued in orderly drawers. Each swatch is searchable through a digital database. A short drive from Akris's St. Gallen headquarters is a warehouse holding thousands of surplus bolts of fabrics that have been developed over the years. From time to time, the warehouse operates as a resource for capsule collections and small orders of special pieces and even for the défilé collection.

"Fabric, in the hundred years of existence of this company, has always been very important," said Peter Kriemler, Akris's president. "It's a type of core value." Maintaining an exacting standard dates back to Alice Kriemler-Schoch, whose taste for St. Gallen embroideries and local noble cottons distinguished her atelier.

Max Kriemler, Albert and Peter's father, inherited his mother's passion for fabrics. When he felt that he could not buy the desired amount of supreme cotton on the market, he founded his own fabric mill and developed fabrics made from fine Swiss cotton.

When Max acquired specialized tailoring ateliers in the 1970s, the Italian-trained sartos brought their knowledge of working with double-face fabrics to achieve exceptional cut and fit. Double-face materials – whether wool, linen, silk, cotton or cashmere – are realized through an extremely thin and fine double-layered weave, a technique that results in mirror-image sides to the fabric. There is no inside and outside, right side or wrong side. Both sides are finished with equal polish and finesse so that the garment can remain unlined, lightweight and supple. Many pieces in the collection are reversible. Key to the desired effect is minimal, almost invisible seaming. To finish a garment, the two layers of the double-face fabric are pulled slightly apart at the edge, turned inward and sewn with improbably delicacy. It is both an art and a craft.

For Albert it all starts with the fabric

Swatches in the fabric archive

Pattern books in the archive

When the tailors construct a jacket out of fine double-face, its symphony of shape, cut and fit are achieved through a sartorial ironing technique as much as through stitching. "That's why when somebody takes such a double-face blazer and undoes it, he is not able to put it back together," said Albert. "There is so much ironing in the seams, which is intrinsic to the fabric quality. The tailor has the precise feeling of how to steam with a certain pressure to create a tailored blazer."

The skill of the tailor goes hand in hand with the level of the fabric. "Albert works specifically with the designers at the mills down to the yarn, down to the weave and the finish," said Peter. The results exceed industry standards, creating de facto exclusives to Akris.

"Fashion is not just visual. It is also tactile, it's about feeling," said Albert. "You have to feel it. When you put this fabric against your skin, you understand." It is true luxury.

When selecting fabrics, Albert always keeps color in mind. "I love color, but in the end, what color you choose is a question of definition and in which fabric the color looks best," he said. "Sometimes a material takes away color intensity." For example, a pure silk in a shade of grass green from the Spring/Summer 2012 collection was chosen because Albert had never seen that shade of green on a fabric. He named it Monaco Green. "Pure silk, pure cashmere, horsehair takes color in an amazing way," he said. "If you do wool in this color it wouldn't work."

Albert's eye for color was awakened when he started doing cruise collections for Akris, which required traveling to different climates, such as the tropical and southern locales of Miami, Dallas and Southern California, where the clients love bright, vivid hues as opposed to the European and East Coast black, beige, white and navy. He travels with a color card in his wallet, taking it out on plane rides to sketch ideas of how to expand the depth and breadth of the Akris palette and which fabrics will be most complementary.

A particular shade of blue that has been a through line in his collections for years originated in 2007 when he wanted to develop a shade that matched the blue of the sea at the Marina Grande on the island of Capri, Italy. "I didn't want royal blue, I didn't want turquoise," Albert said. The shade he was seeking didn't exist on the market so he went into the Akris archive and found a swatch from 1969 from Abraham Silks. He developed Marina Grande blue in wool and silk and has used it in his collections since.

If clients and different climates opened Albert's eyes to the possibility of color, his interest in art accelerated and evolved his sense of it. Egon Schiele's paintings inspired the deep green and blue of the Fall/Winter 2018 Vienna Salonières collection. Romanian artist Geta Brătescu's collage work inspired the pale pink and black pairings of the Spring/Summer 2019 collection. Johann Wolfgang von Goethe's *Theory of Colors* inspired the kaleidoscope prints of Fall/Winter 2019 and an exhibition at the Goethe Museum in Düsseldorf, Germany. Antonio Calderara's paintings of the sunlight in the morning on Lago di Orta, Italy inspired the metallics of the Spring/Summer 2020 collection.

Embroidery archive established by Alice Kriemler-Schoch,
still in use today

Drawers in the fabric archive

Soon-to-be-used fabric panels in the fabric department

Fabric bolts in the storage depot near St. Gallen

"I was intrigued by how concerned Goethe was with the effect of colors on the human psyche," Albert said. "In my work, it is crucial on which fabric a color works best and how a dress affects the wearer's perception of herself. Therefore, the exploration of color in my work is a fundamental one, in the pursuit of new colors and the appreciation and application of the classic colors."

The final chapter in Albert's St. Gallen series for Fall/Winter 2022 is one of the most color-intense collections in Akris's history. The gridded prints depicting the graphic work of Reinhard Voigt, specifically his 1970s and 1980s paintings *Drei Teile*, *The Order of Things #2* and an untitled work, gave Albert a new prism and color spectrum to aspire to. Voigt's work had a modernity Albert set out to capture by rendering his paintings as prints on double-face tailoring, tulle blousons and a color-blocked sequined gown, each fabric chosen to ensure maximum impact for the colors. He worked with his printer of thirty years in Como, Italy, Gianpaolo Ghioldi, to achieve the most true-to-life results.

The range of hues present in Voigt's work, from the pale flesh tone of a woman's face to the pink of her lips to the doe brown of her hair, gave Albert an opportunity to consider a vast range of colors and fabrics within one collection. Gallus green was rendered in a silken neoprene that took on a modern, sporty luster. Pure, undyed camel hair was chosen because it produces a shade of camel that can't be achieved when dying silks or cottons. A cashmere felt developed with Loro Piana was chosen for a specific shade of beige, because "beige is tricky, beige can look very old," said Albert, who likes to challenge himself with one two unlikely colors each season. "What is the balance between blush and nude? Nude is not very flattering. You need to be extra chic to wear nude well," he said, picking up a swatch that had just the right ratio of pink to create a blush nude that instantly flatters whoever wears it. It's a chic game to play indeed.

Silk and chenille jacquard, satin duchesse

A VISION OF A MODERN WOMAN, Salle Soufflot, Le Carrousel du Louvre   The collection is about a change in attitude. It is about precision, clean lines and sharper silhouettes. Each piece in the collection is a statement while also being understated – just as the woman who wears it would like to appear. I don't want her to waste precious time thinking of what she's wearing, regardless of the occasion. I want to give her that feeling that, when you slip into an Akris suit or dress – you're done. And cashmere and silk seemed to be the perfect fabrics for it.

Alpaca (fleece) with satin duchesse, grosgrain stretch velvet

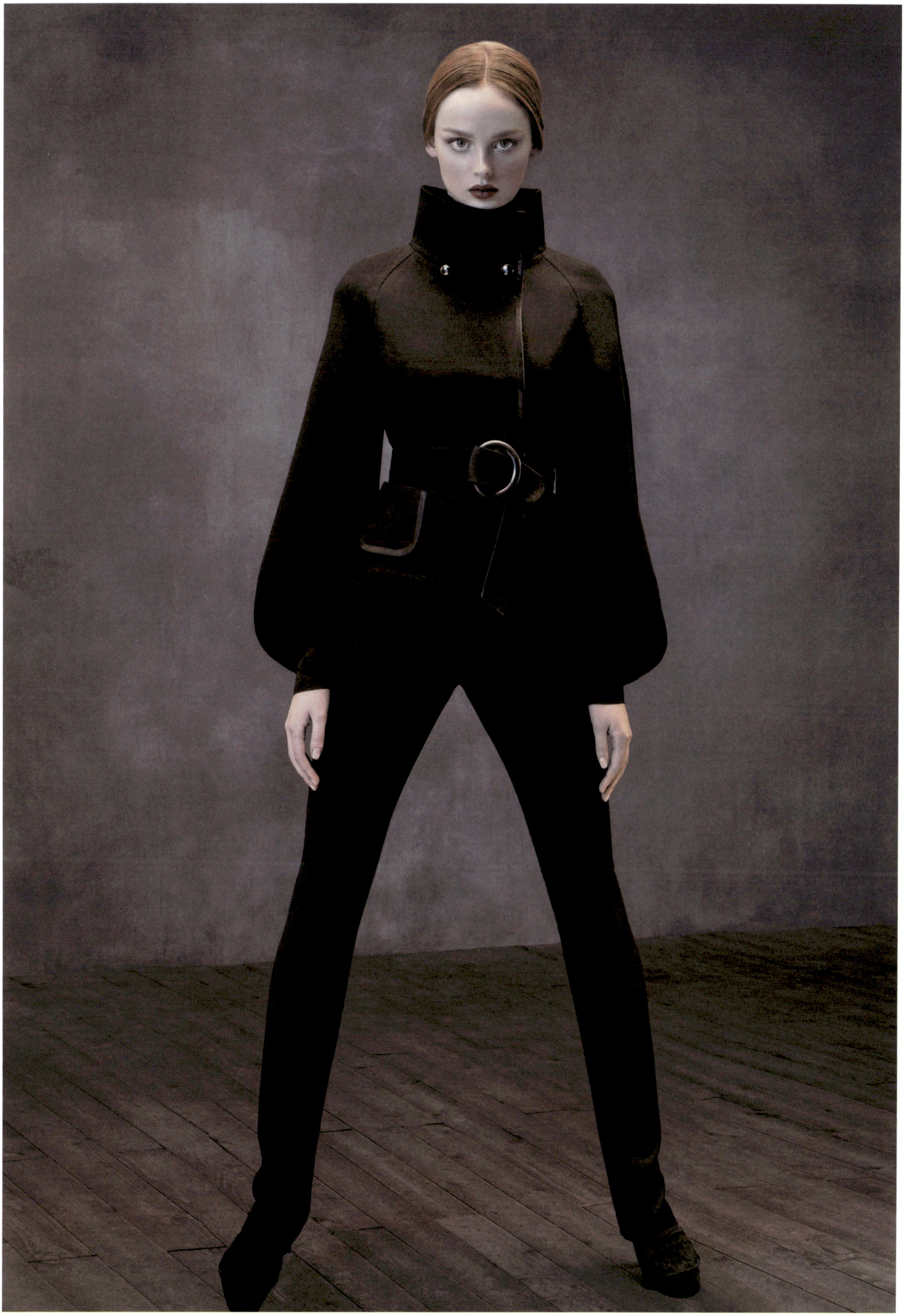

Light cashmere double-face, wool double-face

Camel hair double-face, silk rib knit

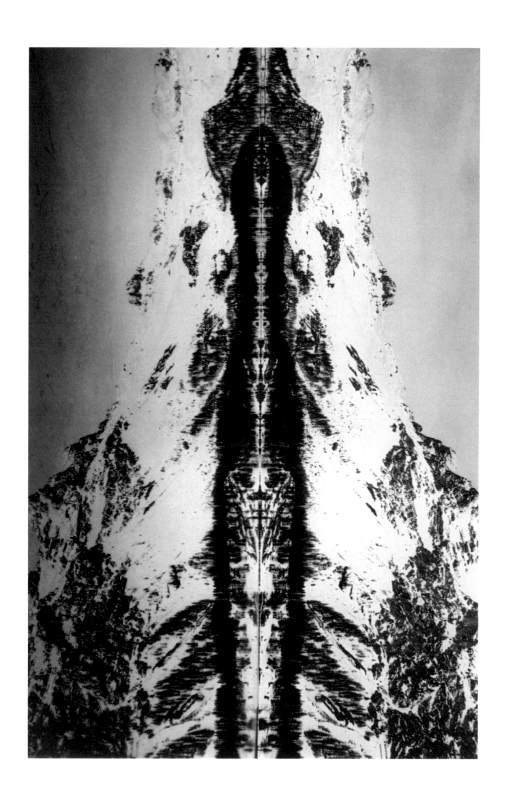

DOUBLE-FACE IS AKRIS'S HERITAGE, Palais de Chaillot   A collection based on sleek tailoring with feminine touches, embracing the sensuousness of fabrics. It was all about comfort and fashion, the nonchalance of super-soft camel hair parkas and elongated tweed suits, based on the winter mood of a photograph I found by Swiss artist Barbara Hée. It is named after Chaviolas, an island in Lake Sils in Engadine. We turned it on its side, and printed in the length of a dress. People were congratulating us on this Rorschach Test print, and it was actually a forest mirrored in a lake. I like fashion to surprise.

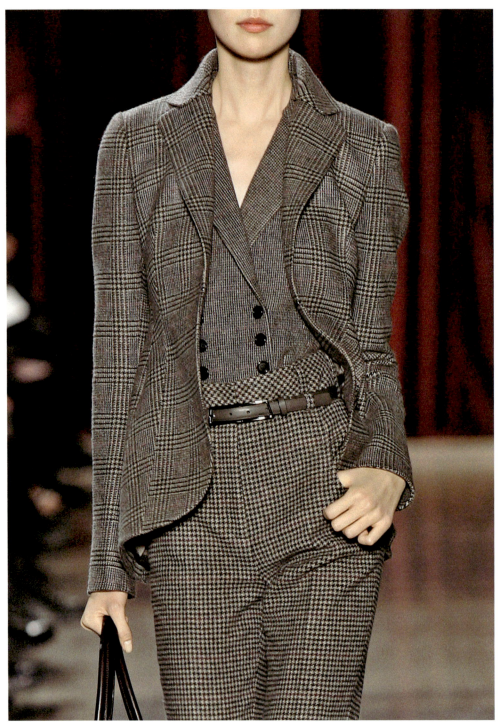

Cashmere prince-de-galles, cashmere fil-à-fil, cashmere pied-de-poule

Double-Face Is Akris's Heritage

Jersey/silk Mountain Lake print

ALBERT KRIEMLER × IAN HAMILTON FINLAY, Salle Delorme, Le Carrousel du Louvre   I wanted to do a collection on the poet and garden artist Ian Hamilton Finlay, but I didn't quite know how to approach his work. I remembered two pictures I had taken during my visit to his home in Scotland: one of his beloved glade in the forest, and the other of the water lilies in his pond. Some months earlier, in Lucerne, I had spotted one of the first inkjet printers that could print photos on fabric. We printed the images on matte sequins developed by Jakob Schlaepfer. At our show the surprising and novel vibrancy of the looks revealed itself – and I discovered the significance of photo prints for our future. The little forest of real Black Olive trees onstage created a magic atmosphere that evoked the artist's garden.

Handcrafted net in silk satin duchesse

Albert Kriemler × Ian Hamilton Finlay

Water Lily digital print on matte sequins

Glade digital print on step-pleated silk georgette

Cotton double-face

A SCIENTIST'S DREAM OF NATURE, Grand Palais   The natural world – its flora and fauna, its landscapes and geology. As I grew up near the mountains, I feel attracted to nature, and to a greater or lesser extent my work is always informed by nature. The collection manifests my appreciation for natural fibers. We worked with intense textural play through nature-based motifs like honeycomb and algae. Simple, subtle, eminently desirable.

Line print on cotton voile/jersey

Cotton Seagrass St. Gallen embroidery

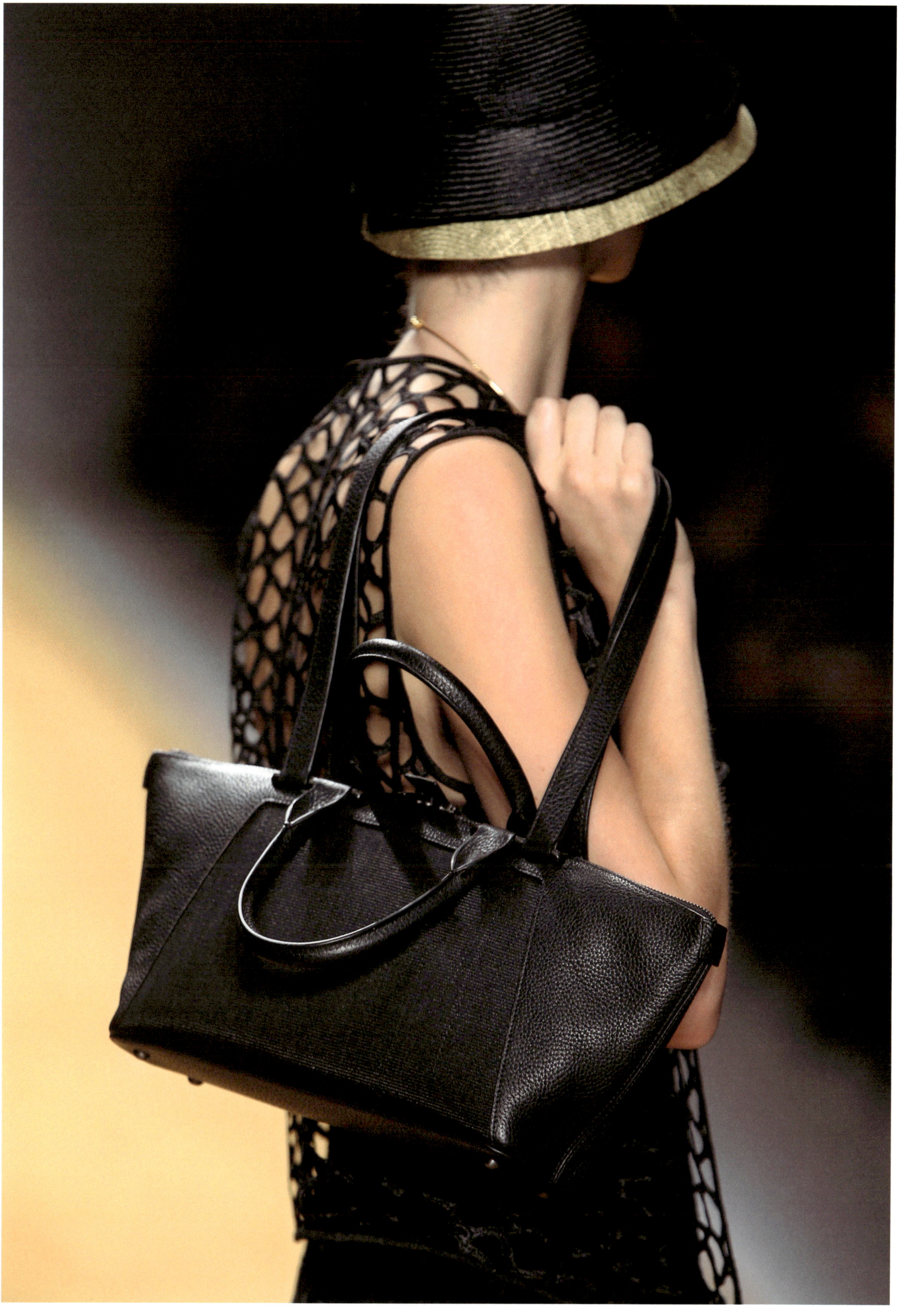

Honeycomb St. Gallen embroidery

Silk georgette and tulle inset, cashmere knit

WIENER WERKSTÄTTE, Salle Soufflot, Le Carrousel de Louvre   The ornate style favored by the Wiener Werkstätte seemed almost anti-Akris at first, but I liked the idea of including details in a discreet way. I was especially interested in the Zurich branch of the Wiener Werkstätte and the materials they used such as Galalith, as well as this fantastic Japanese-influenced wallpaper pattern designed by the Austrian artist Dagobert Peche. The Wiener Werkstätte always placed great emphasis on materials, and I can relate to that. But if the materials are rich, you must keep the design clean. We wanted to play on that tension between refinement and simplicity.

Cashmere/wool double-face with wool border and printed lining

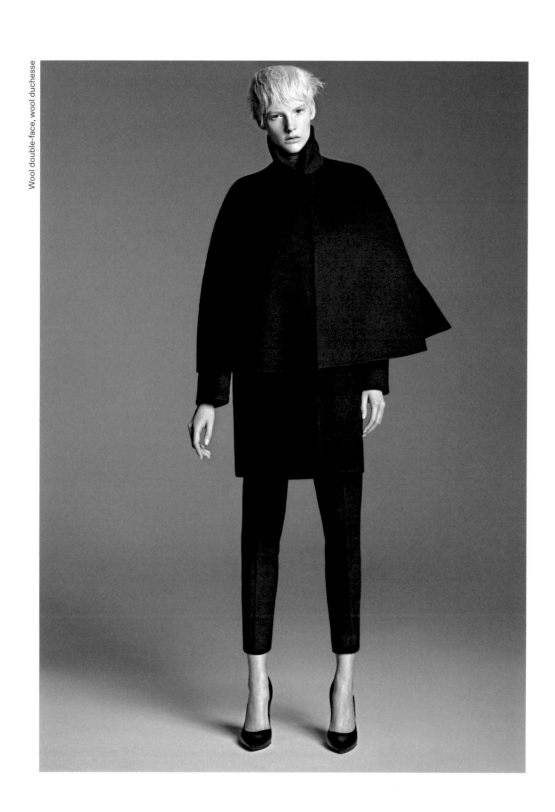

Wool double-face, wool duchesse

A TRIBUTE TO MY MOTHER, UTE KRIEMLER, Grand Palais   My mother Ute was the most elegant woman I have met in my life and she is a constant inspiration to this very day. She embodied Akris in so many ways. When she passed away in 2012, I decided to create a collection inspired by her personal wardrobe: her beloved turtlenecks, translated into tulle and elongated into short dresses, her blouse-and-pant combinations, and an overall sleek sportiness. A twenty-piece chamber orchestra conducted by composer Thomas Roussel in an all-white set played music by her favorite composer: Bach.

Who Would Have Guessed It's Embroidery?

Design teams from Paris and Milan regularly travel to St. Gallen to develop new ideas. From Akris, the trip is much shorter

By Jessica Iredale

A tour of Forster Rohner's headquarters, perched on a hill overlooking the valley of St. Gallen, encompasses the full scope of the town's history as the capital of the world's finest embroideries. The company's library houses stacks upon stacks of books containing embroidery samples dating back to the late 1800s, well before what is now Forster Rohner was founded in 1904 by Conrad Forster-Willi as Forster Willi & Co. The pages include embroideries crafted for Cristóbal Balenciaga in the 1960s, Hubert de Givenchy in the 1970s – photographed by a then unknown Helmut Newton – and present-day Prada. The design headquarters is busy at work for lingerie clients the world over, as well as for some of the most prestigious fashion houses in Paris and Milan – and, of course, Akris.

Things have evolved significantly since Emanuel's great-grandfather founded Forster Rohner, at a time when St. Gallen was an embroidery boomtown. "This was the area for embroidery worldwide," says Emanuel. "In France, you have lace. Here, you have embroidery." The region's history with textiles dates back to the twelfth century, when eastern Switzerland became a thriving center for the production of woven linen, which brought great prosperity to the region. By the mid-eighteenth century, cotton had replaced linen as the fabric of choice. Eventually the global market for cotton became increasingly crowded and St. Gallen pivoted to specializing in delicate cotton embroideries, a status symbol among the affluent class, who used embroidered fabrics for their clothes, accessories and homes. By 1910, embroidery was Switzerland's biggest export.

Conrad Forster-Willi was working for one of the many other local embroidery firms when he decided to go the independent route and established Forster Rohner in 1904. The period spanning the First World War, the Great Depression and the Second World War wreaked havoc on the world economy, with the Swiss embroidery industry no exception. Once flush with local businesses and healthy competition, the industry contracted sharply. Yet Forster Rohner persevered, developing close relationships with the Parisian haute couture houses throughout the 1940s. "My grandfather worked very closely with those people," says Emanuel. "He was really a designer but with a good business sense. This is still our heritage today." Design teams from Milan and Paris regularly make trips to Forster Rohner's St. Gallen headquarters as well as to other St. Gallen embroiderers such as Bischoff to study the archives and develop new ideas for broderie anglaise, guipure and sequined embroidery.

For Albert Kriemler, the trip is much shorter. Instead of dispatching his design team, he often visits personally to create innovative embroideries and experiment with new ideas. The Kriemler and Forster families go back decades, their relationship built not only on steady business but also a shared culture and St. Gallen pride. There is no Akris collection without St. Gallen embroidery.

"We have seen all the floral, very heavy style," says Emanuel. "Of course, people like it. But Albert finds ways to work with it in a modern way with a geometric, more architectural style." The signature trapezoidal A embroidery that has become shorthand for the house is one example

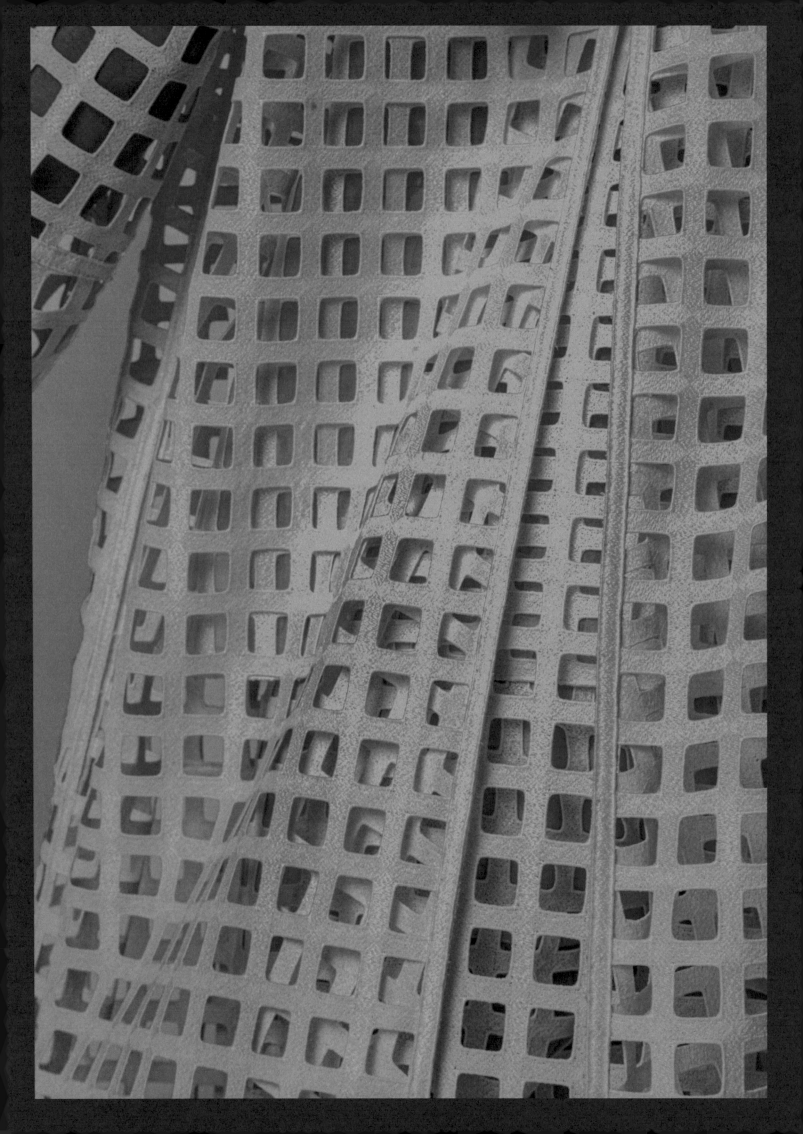

of Albert's modern eye. Even more avant-garde are the luminescent, glow-in-the-dark sequins used for Akris's eveningwear. Then there's the flashing LED embroidery crafted with a conductive thread called e-broidery®, which is trademarked by Forster Rohner. Embroidered onto silk crêpe, the thread is powered by a battery pack that's worn hidden in the pocket of the gowns and suits. For his Fall/Winter 2014 collection, done in collaboration with artist Thomas Ruff, Albert uused the LED embroidery on a tuxedo, gowns and the Ai bag to create a starry night-sky effect inspired by Ruff's work. This was the first industrial integration of a flashing light technology on a fabric that will keep its elasticity and drape, and can withstand dry cleaning and machine washing. Pieces from the collection are part of the permanent collection of the MAK – Museum of Applied Arts, Vienna.

A feat of imagination, innovation and partnership between two St. Gallen-based, family-owned institutions, the LED embroidery is a testament to creativity, craft and the Swiss excellence shared by Akris and Forster Rohner. Embroidery is an ancient craft and can also be completely modern. As Albert said of the Fall/Winter 2016 collection and its chunky Elephant embroidery, "I think St. Gallen embroidery has almost infinite potential for a very modern look and can be so much more than what you might expect. In that oversized sweater dress, so much volume is added to the fabric. Who would have guessed it's embroidery?"

SAVANNAH RED, Grand Palais   Simply red, blended in a dazzle of African prints. On a family trip to Kenya and Tanzania, I discovered Africa's red earth. Red is everything from orange to aubergine. It means love, passion. And there is nothing that heightens your senses more than the diversity of life on this impressive continent. We translated it into a richness of fabrics. A leather scale embellishment was so finely rendered that it almost tricked the eye into believing it was actual python skin.

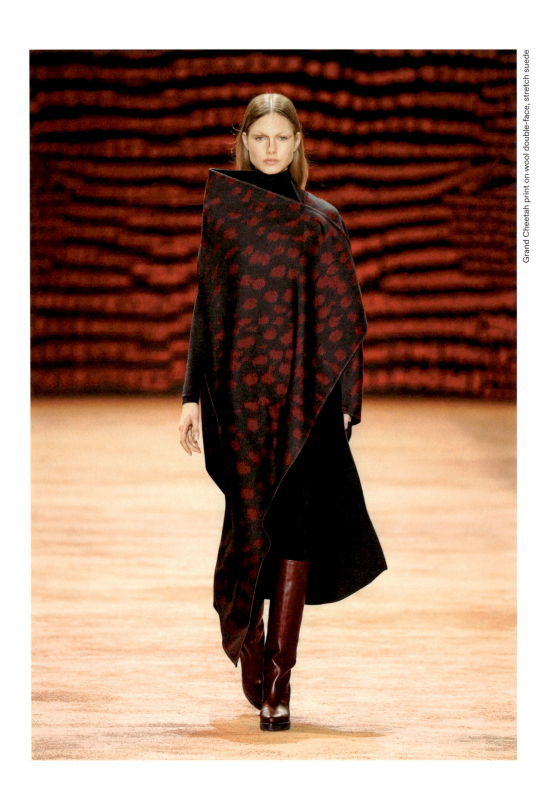

Grand Cheetah print on wool double-face, stretch suede

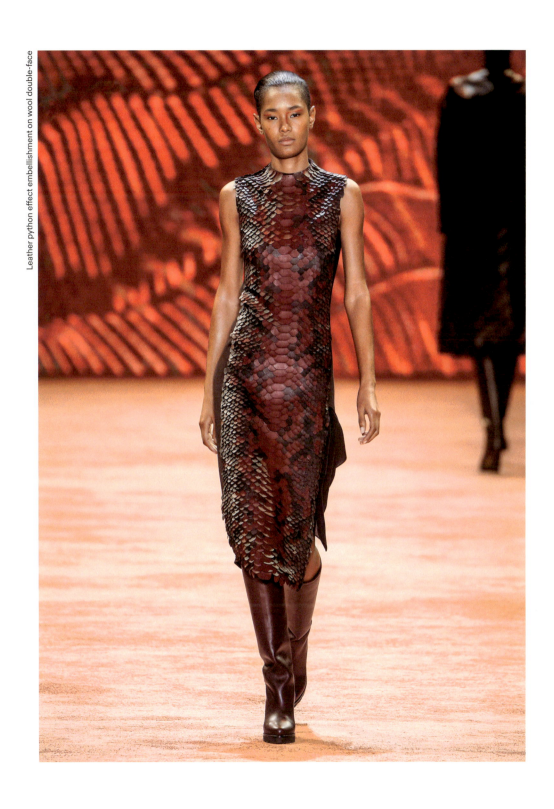

Leather python effect embellishment on wool double-face

Savannah Red

FÉLIX VALLOTTON, Akris Showroom, Paris   Our first défilé in Paris. I was looking for a concept to add value to my collection other than it being my new clothes. Then, one rainy weekend, I saw the collection of artist Félix Vallotton's work at Villa Flora in Winterthur, Switzerland, and was captivated by his colors, by the way he treated light. The colors were rich without being loud. That cassis, and then there was the green. On a different note, I was made aware about the story with the artists from Les Nabis; Vallotton was the only Swiss in the Parisian group that, more than a hundred years ago, redefined painting. As a Swiss designer coming to Paris, I was quite sympathetic.

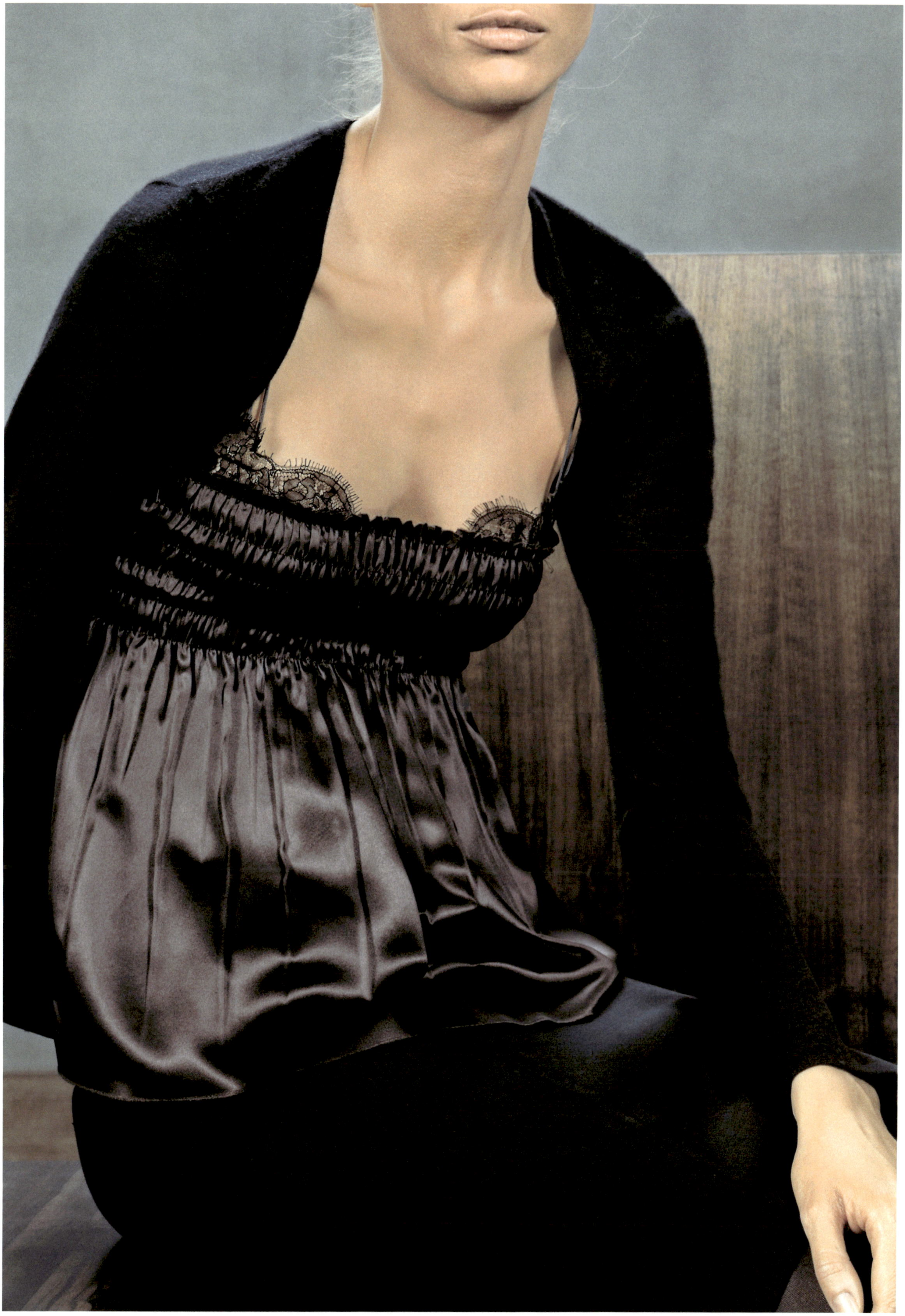

Cashmere/silk knit, silk satin with lace insets

Faces print on water-repellent silk taffeta

ALBERT KRIEMLER × ALEXANDER GIRARD, Palais de Tokyo   A universe of love and delight. In 2016, I saw an exhibition about Alexander Girard, one of the twentieth century's most gifted design visionaries, curated by the Vitra Design Museum. I came to see it again twice more, as I was so excited by his genius sense of color. In Santa Fe, New Mexico, I met his family and saw his vast folk art collection. It sparked a collection of Southern Modernism: breezy suits, chiffon dresses and accessories in strong colors and patterns. Roman Numerals in 3-D rubber for bags, Double Hearts embroidering love – and a Wooden Doll print on a giant Wooden Doll stage.

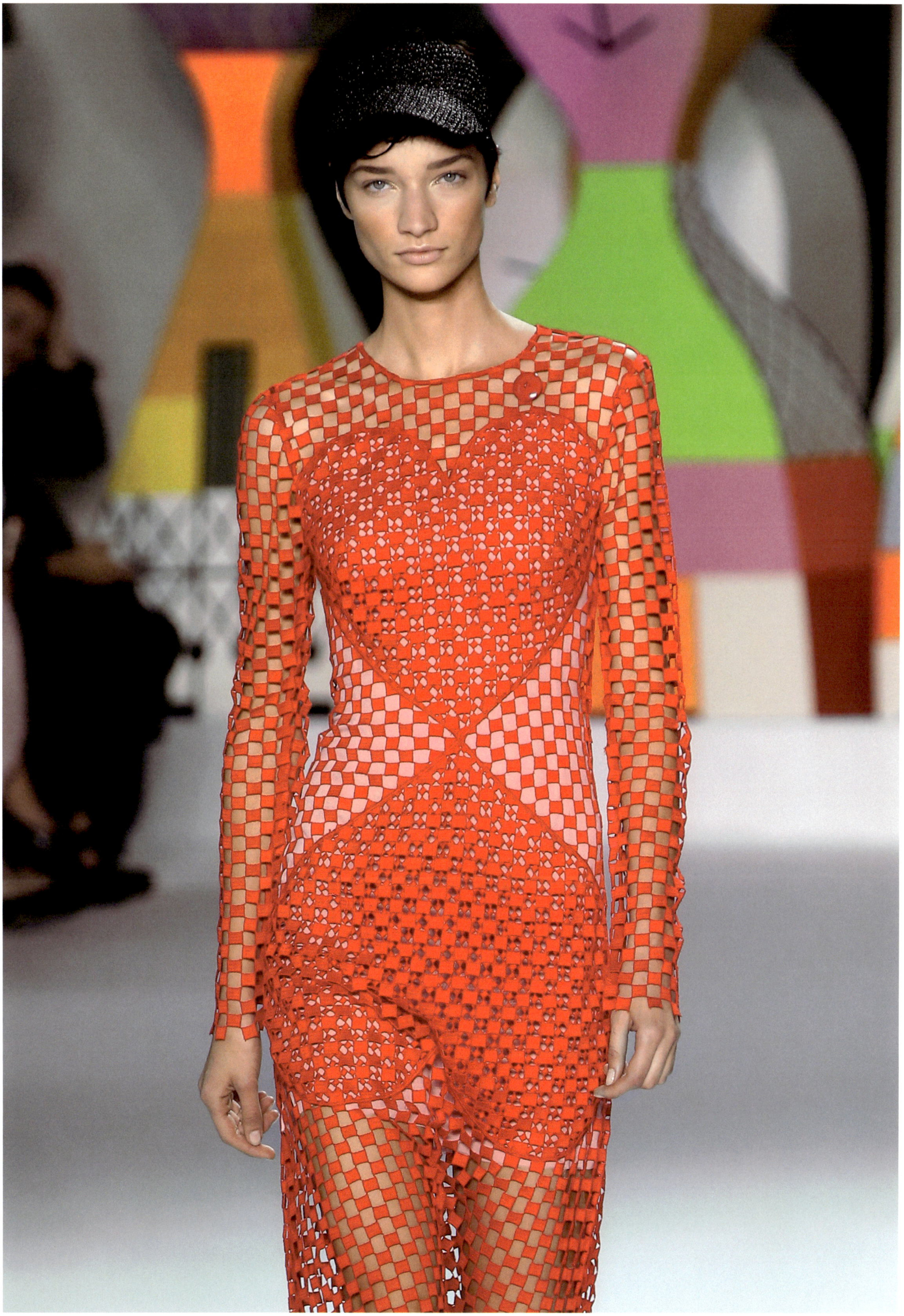

Double Heart cotton St. Gallen embroidery

Wooden Doll print on silk crêpe georgette

Albert Kriemler × Alexander Girard

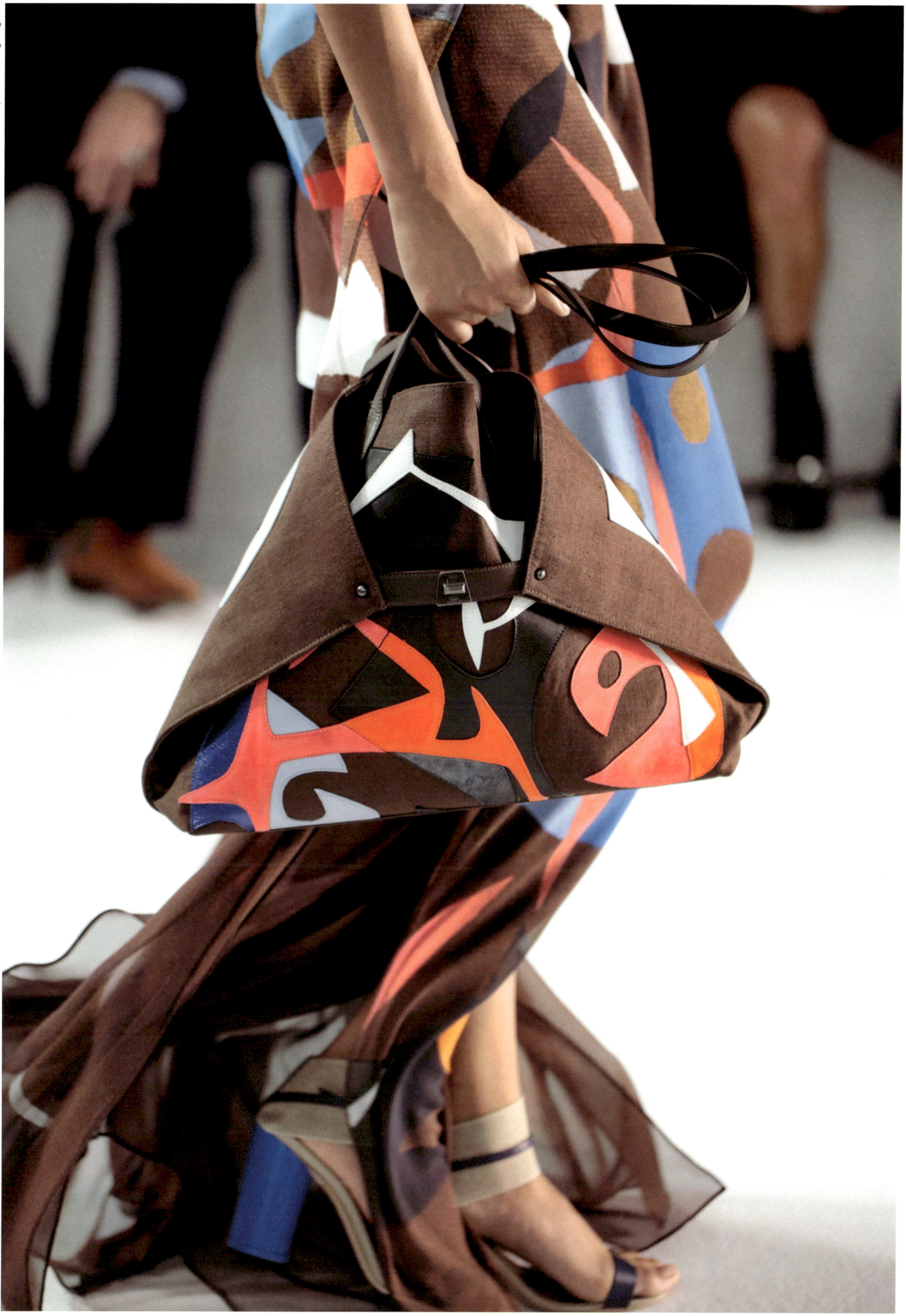

Masonite print on silk georgette

Silk georgette

CELEBRATING TEN YEARS OF AI, Grand Palais   When I designed the first Ai bag, the idea was to fold a classic tote into a trapezoidal silhouette. With this in mind, I created layered, simple looks for a collection inspired by how the Ai is folding. To celebrate the occasion, we built a giant 10-meter-high silver version of the Ai as a backdrop, out of which the models marched in scintillating fabrics and iridescent paillettes. They were inspired by the paintings of Italian artist Antonio Calderara, who spectacularly captured the energy that only sunlight on water can trigger. Pictured is a print based on his painting *Spazio Luce*.

Mezzo Mezzo print on cotton/silk double-face and silk crêpe

Cotton guipure, crinkle silk organza

GIORGIO MORANDI, Salle Soufflot, Le Carrousel du Louvre   The dusty beiges and smoky taupes of Italian artist Giorgio Morandi always fascinated me. I already knew I wanted to do pastels, and I went to Bologna to see an exhibition of his perfect still lifes. What I took home was this blurred light. It was an autumn day, a bit hazy; and in Morandi's paintings, the colors were like a feeling of mist. They made me think of tulle and layers of chiffon cloqué, organza and transparent gossamer lace for a subtle look of seduction.

Kaleidoscope print on wool double-face, cashmere/jersey

MAKE YOUR MARK!, Grand Palais   Eight horsehair exclamation marks by Richard Artschwager. A perfect symbol for uniqueness and strength. I dedicated this collection to horsehair, the signature fabric of Akris accessories, and to the women of today making their mark (surprisingly superb in Goethe's magical *Farbtafel* series prints). As fabrics are key to the tactile universe I want to create, we narrowed the runway and had front seats only to better include the audience in the conversation between a woman and her clothes.

Colorama print on silk crêpe de chine

Wool double-face

AI. THE LAUNCH OF THE FIRST AKRIS HANDBAG, Musée de l'Homme   Timeless. Architectural. For every occasion. Morning to evening. Just like the Ai, our first handbag made of rarefied horsehair. The image of a woman on the move was the motif while we were designing this collection. Clean was the motto; sportswear elements the key. Net in leather, nylon in a double-face jacket; juxtaposing tailored and sensual, defined and soft.

The Ai Bag

By Jessica Iredale

A quiet yet rich story of understatement, craft and history is woven into the Ai bag, the Akris signature first introduced in fall 2009. It begins with the silhouette, a trapezoid derived from the letter A, the initial from which the company descends – A for Akris, A for Albert, A for Ai. Devoid of overt logos, the trapezoid telegraphs the house identity with the utmost subtlety.

Definitive in silhouette, the Ai bag is further distinguished by its unique material of choice – horsehair, a fiber rare in its refinement, lightweight durability and inherent sustainability. Each Ai bag requires hair from the tails of two horses, woven in the course of two days. The hair is sourced from wild Mongolian horses who roam free, their tails and manes shorn in a ceremonial tradition and allowed to regrow over a two-year, all-natural process.

Albert Kriemler had used the material in tailoring to add refined structure to jackets, as well as in interior design. Each Akris showroom and boutique is set with a horsehair-covered wall. The brilliance and depth of hue that can be achieved through horsehair, each fiber absorbing the dye to its own degree to create a lustrous intensity and dimension, appealed to Albert's sense of color. He was intrigued when approached by a German atelier specializing in horsehair accessories.

In 2008, Akris acquired the atelier, the exceptional know-how of its craftsmen and, along with it, the relationship with one of the last mills able to weave horse-hair on its looms from the late nineteenth century. The inimitable properties of horsehair and the possible range of palette it offers satisfied Albert's desire to launch accessories with a distinct fabric. Ai bags have been designed in more than fifty colors and five metallic hues. The bag is convertible and can be opened into a classic tote or folded into its signature trapezoid secured with a delicate strap. It is trimmed in Italian leather.

Ai bags are offered in leather, embroidery, fabric or neoprene. But no material compares to horsehair. "It was an unexpected fabric in luxury accessories when I chose horsehair for the first Ai bag," Albert Kriemler says. "It is a historical material but its properties make it look like it could have been designed for just now. It is perfect for travel, as it is much lighter and more resilient than leather, and it is animal-friendly. The colors get more beautiful with time and use. And it is so rare. To me, horsehair represents a new era of handbag refinement." Then there's the name. Chosen in homage to a famous Japanese horse, the name Ai translates to "love."

Following pages: The trapezoidal architecture
of the Ai bag captured by Iwan Baan

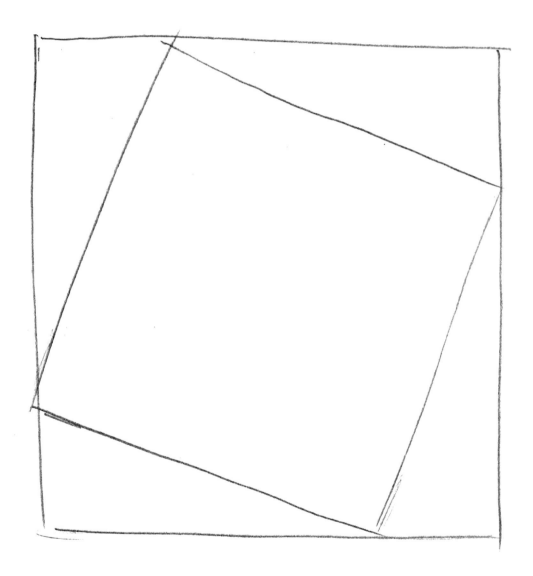

KAZIMIR MALEVICH, Grand Palais   Celebrating independence. A visit to *Malevich: Revolutionary of Russian Art* at London's Tate Modern, marking the centenary of the artist's groundbreaking 1915 exhibit, reminded me of how he liberated art from representing reality. He created his famous *Black Square* and left interpretations up to viewers' imaginations. What an independent mind. Squares are a recurrent element in my fashion vernacular and here I wanted to place an element of pure individualism into the collection through simple geometric forms, as shown in a sketch I made, and shades of black and white.

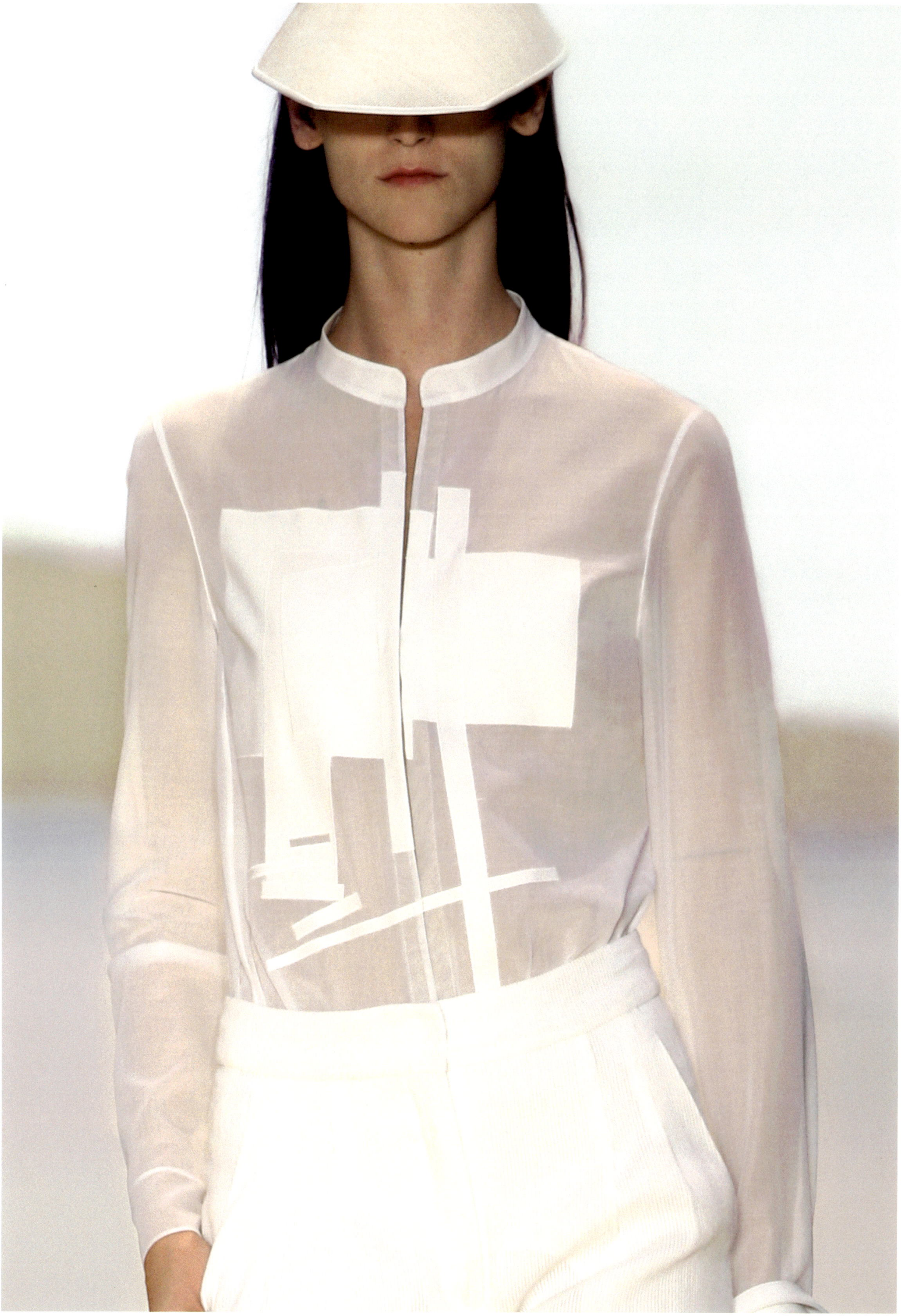

Satin and poplin patchwork on cotton voile

Wool double-face on tulle

Spring/Summer 2015

Reversible nappa leather, satin and poplin patchwork on cotton voile, nappa leather

Net embroidery, jersey, silk taffeta

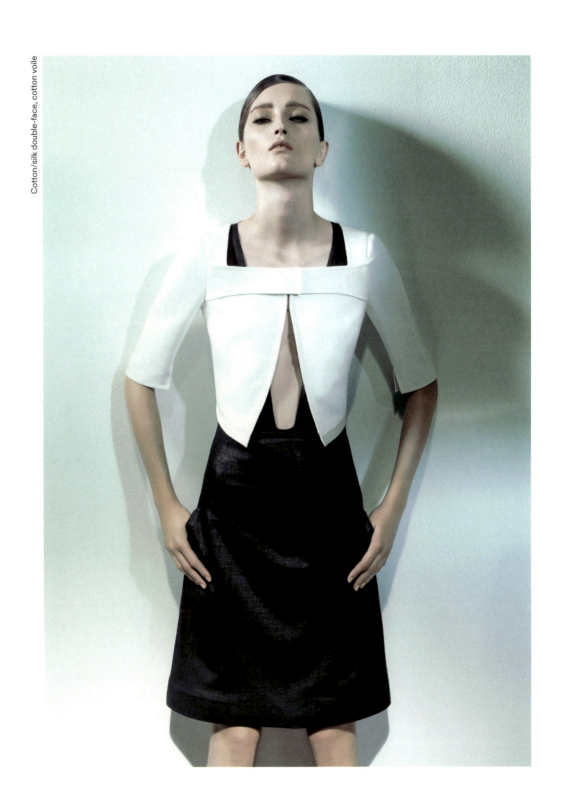

Cotton/silk double-face, cotton voile

IT'S ALL ABOUT TRANSPARENCY, Salle Delorme, Le Carrousel du Louvre   The starting point was a Rudi Gernreich swimsuit from my vintage archive. Its clean lines and graphic simplicity stunned me. It is part of each look. Worn back to front, and front to back. In stretch cotton or almost invisible nude tulle. The collection is all about transparency, about what you think you see. Or don't see. Body-conscious, feminine, but in new proportions and unexpected volumes.

Silk tulle with applied graduated stripes of felted cashmere

AKRIS PER SE, Salle Delorme, Le Carrousel du Louvre   Fashion should enhance rather than hide a woman's natural grace and strength, so you see the woman first. For this collection we eliminated anything superfluous to show the quiet power of Akris tailoring: ease and a relaxed elegance. A versatile wardrobe with signature pieces like a cashmere double-face suit or a sleek, flattering dress, updated by color, cut and choice of fabric. Fashion emphasizing tactile sensuality. Fashion for the independent, modern woman.

Cashmere/silk jersey

Camel hair double-face, flannel, suede

The Women Who Wear Akris

An understanding of how modern women live is at the core of Akris. Five such women ponder on how wearing Akris makes them feel

By Jessica Iredale

When Indra Nooyi discovered Akris in 2010, four years after she had been named CEO of PepsiCo, she was one of eleven female CEOs of a Fortune 500 company. Her first purchase was the Akris double-face sheath. She bought three or four of the same style in black, navy and gray so each dress could be paired with multiple jackets.

"If you look at my closet now, it's about 65 percent Akris," said Nooyi, who cherishes the exquisite tailoring and fit of the clothes, not to mention the boost of confidence they provided to the lone senior-ranking woman in rooms dominated by men.

"No longer did I have to feel uncomfortable about the fact that I was a woman or an immigrant or a person of color," said Nooyi. "There I was, this elegantly turned-out person. They say clothes make the man. I tell you something, clothes make a woman too, if they're the right clothes." Albert Kriemler can hardly take credit for her success, but neither would argue that he provided the right clothes for her.

Women have always been the core of Akris, from the house's founder Alice Kriemler-Schoch, whose entrepreneurial spirit and exacting elegance defined the company's DNA, to Ute Kriemler, whose subtlety and grace cemented lasting relationships with clients and stores. Her memory and presence still loom large. "Albert Kriemler's effortlessly dressed, elegant and sportif mother Ute was always at the heart of the brand, not only in her style but also in her utter ease, confidence and timeless appeal," said Linda Fargo, Senior Vice President of Fashion at Bergdorf Goodman. "She was Albert's muse to be sure, and at the core of his inspiration for many years."

As she steered her sons to take over the family business, Ute was key to Akris's relationship to Bergdorf Goodman, which began in 1988 and continues today. She was the company's envoy to New York, hosting trunk shows and sales appointments with all the department stores in the eighties and nineties. The personal touch of a family-held fashion brand, tended to by its personal custodians, made Akris a rarity. "Ute would be there in the sales meeting waiting to greet you. She would walk you through," said Roopal Patel, Fashion Director of Saks Fifth Avenue.

This personal touch and familial commitment to excellence is literally in the fiber of the brand, in Fargo's opinion. "Every time I am able to go the showroom itself, and touch the ultra-luxe materials, observe the subtle and innovative architecture of each piece, relish the innovations in the fabrics and engineering, I am reminded of what 'luxury' really means, at a time when the very word is bantered about without earning it," she says. "It's Albert who seeks and creates these fabrications and constructions. He doesn't hesitate. He's so utterly sure of himself, and his complete understanding of the Akris woman and her changing life. His output is prolific and astounding. What he, with his brother Peter, and their family have built is both remarkable and very rare."

"What distinguishes Akris is design that's focused on clear lines, but really with this creative and modern flair," said Lana Todorovich, President and Chief Merchandising Officer of Neiman Marcus. "Then you

add very luxurious fabrications – exceptional embroideries and laces that often are in graphic, dramatic shapes – and then you add colors, which is something our clients really love and appreciate and take joy in." Then there's the touch, the exceptional tactile hand of the clothes. Todorovich was struck by a sky-blue cashmere coat from the Fall/Winter 2022 collection during a walk-through in the Akris showroom. "It was gorgeous in itself, but then when you touch it, the cashmere just makes you kind of fall in love on multiple levels," she said.

When Patel was at Bergdorf Goodman in the early 2000s, word was circulating about sophisticated minimalist tailoring coming out of the quiet Swiss house. "The rumor was, Albert knew how to cut an incredible jacket," Patel said. She remembers the cut stood out, as well as Albert's architectural lens and way of translating sculptural proportions into his silhouettes. At a time when other designers were working in pinstripes, black, navy and charcoal, he was experimenting with saturated jewel tones, changing up the notch on the collar.

Vanessa Kingori, MBE, Chief Business Officer of Condé Nast Britain bought her first Akris jacket at the London store in 2010 when she was appointed as brand lead for GQ. It was a black jacket with slightly cropped sleeves. As the first woman, the first person of color and the youngest person to ever hold the role, she wanted to make an impression. She sought a piece of clothing that felt empowering and grown-up, feminine, non-conforming and something that didn't feel like she was borrowing from the boys.

She remembers wearing the jacket to her first big meeting as publisher of GQ. Its architectural fit, structured yet not stiff, made Kingori feel that "I was standing up straighter," she said. "That was a really pivotal moment in my life. When you're the first and only in a role like that, you have slight imposter syndrome no matter how qualified you are. There are moments in the day where you think, 'Oh my God, can I do this? Is there a reason that a woman hasn't done this before?' That jacket gave me the feeling of holding me up and making me stand taller." It didn't make the woman – it did what it was designed to do.

Perforated leather, structured silk organza, cotton poplin, cotton double-face

SENSIBILITY & LIGHTNESS, Salle Soufflot, Le Carrousel du Louvre   A portrait of Anjelica Huston, shot by Richard Avedon in the 1970s, was an inspiration for this collection. I loved the whole attitude of it: the blush color of the blouse, which is just a shade darker than Huston's skin, and the treatment of pleated chiffon in the blouse. That season I went lighter than ever before, in airy constructions, with less color, but beautiful tones of nude, rosewood and smoke. The look was feminine. Very feminine.

Silk chiffon

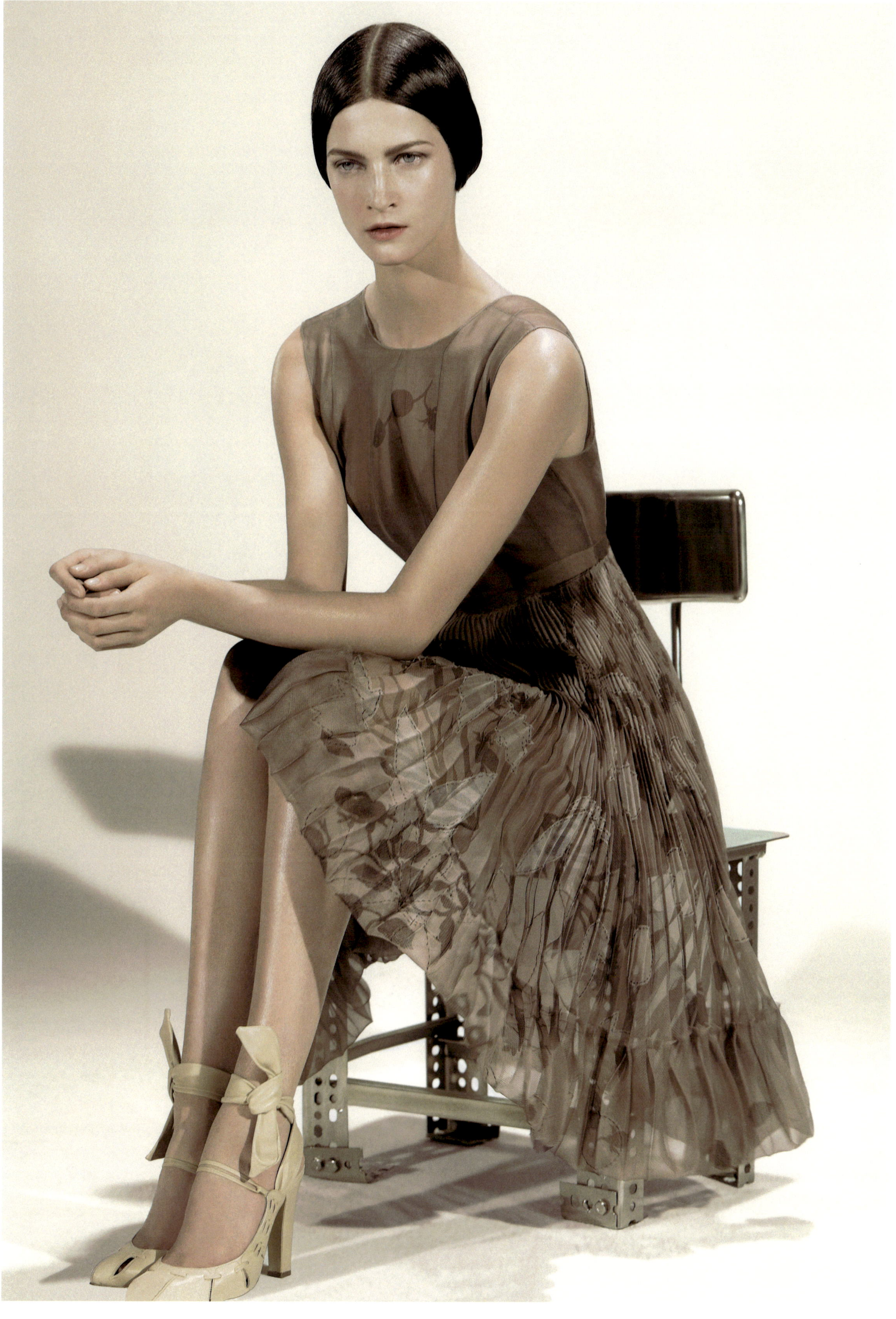
Silk organza and tulle applications on plissé

VIENNA 1900–1918, Palais de Tokyo They came from the future. Madame d'Ora – who captured dancer Elsie Altmann-Loos (pictured) –, Alma Mahler-Werfel and Berta Zuckerkandl, three visionary patronesses of art in Vienna at the beginning of the twentieth century, when Modernism was born. These women in their revolutionary loose, bohemian dresses by Emilie Flöge advocated an independent life and the new art by Egon Schiele and Gustav Klimt. My collections have always been created for women who make a difference. This one celebrates women's ability to see the new.

Silk crêpe georgette with python application

Stadtbahn St. Gallen embroidery

Wool mix marble jacquard, lace

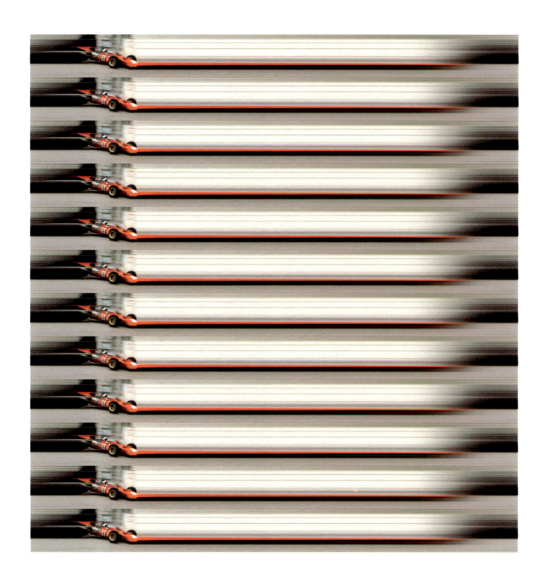

GRAND PRIX OF MONACO, Palais de Chaillot   The spirit of girls' and boys' clothes in John Frankenheimer's movie *Grand Prix*. The high-pitched whirr of Formula One racing cars, and Princess Charlene of Monaco as a muse of the moment. In 2011, I had designed clothes for her for the first time, and she immediately understood that Akris is more than what meets the eye. She inspired this collection of easy, elegant shapes and sporty attitude. A year later she wore our Grand Prix dress with little race cars to the Formula One race.

Grand Prix print on silk marocain

Lace stripe

Lace stripe

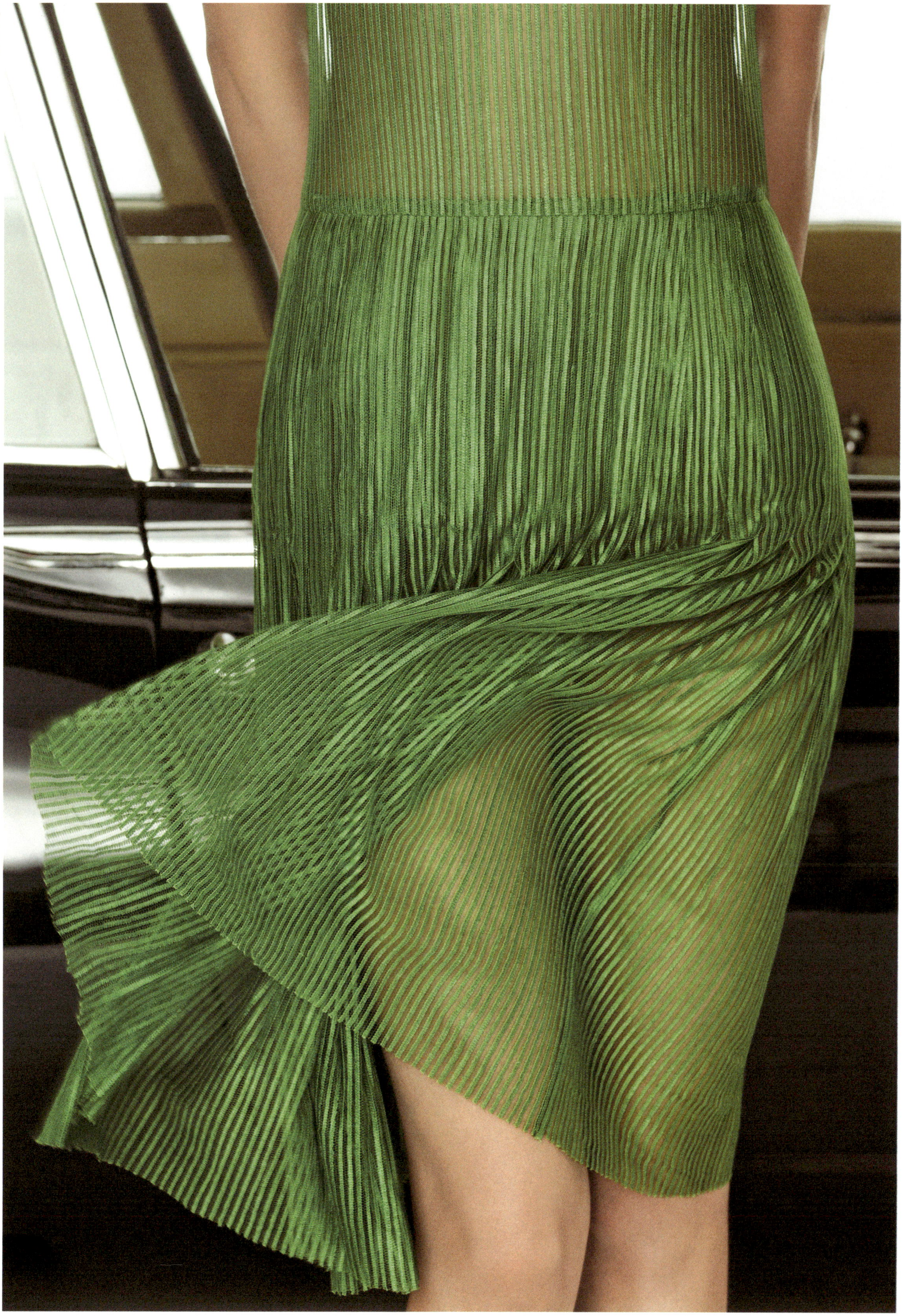

TOGETHER WE CREATE, Musée d'Art Moderne de Paris   The French architect Robert Mallet-Stevens and his community of creative minds, the Union des artistes modernes, who made Paris a capital of avant-garde, were the inspiration for a collection of cubist volumes and orphism patterns. I admire how daringly they erased the boundaries between art and crafts. After all, we create together. I am working with our fabulous tailors, pattern-makers, print, fabric and embroidery collaborators. Our transparent Trapezoid Trees were inspired by Mallet-Stevens' friends, the Martel brothers. To present this collection in the Musée d'Art Moderne de Paris was a stellar moment for all of us.

Silk twill, wool/silk

The Masters

It is the designer who steps out to take the applause at the end of shows at Paris Fashion Week. But a collection is always a collective achievement. In virtually every interview, Albert Kriemler underlines the importance of the team he works closely with every day when creating each collection. He has never seen himself as the manager of a design team, but rather as the creative center and driving force of a community, the members of which are all masters of their trade: pattern-makers, tailors, cutters, knitters, bag-makers. Drawing on their experience, mastery and imagination, their creativity is manifested in their deft transfer of drawings, sketches or ideas into the three-dimensional form of a jacket, a coat or a pair of pants, thus transforming inspiration into a real-world format. Without these people and their interactions, a collection would remain theoretical, wishful thinking only. They are part of the design, from the initial idea to the finished piece: a huge responsibility that is also a source of inspiration. Every collection is a teamwork of experts who bring technique, experience and creativity to the table. Nine of Albert's closest collaborators talk about their craft and what fascinates them in their work.

Following pages: Portraits by Iwan Baan

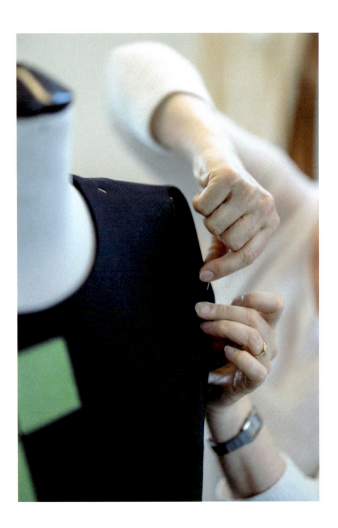

Regina Marending, Pattern-Maker for Dresses and Skirts
With Akris since: 1987

Akris has geometric or abstract lines throughout the designs, but the body has curves all over the place. I ensure that those lines harmonize with the shape of the body, so that the lines stay geometric, vertical or horizontal when the garment is worn, while making sure the bust is worked into the design and everything sits properly. I'm good at that and it's also something I enjoy.

Pattern-makers like me are involved from the outset, when the design team is still considering the theme. We can already contribute technical expertise at that stage.

I find it fascinating to receive a two-dimensional sketch and a fabric and consider how to realize this idea as a three-dimensional prototype, using this material, plus my technical skills, experience and creativity. Then I come up with my solution and put it into practice during the fittings with Albert.

We're also in charge of grading the pattern to ensure that the fit is right in all sizes. That means we are involved throughout the process until the garment is completed.

Severin Meyer, Pattern-Maker for Blazers and Jackets

With Akris since: 1997

I want to tame the fabric and realize beautiful proportions and lines with it. After all, the Akris philosophy is "less is more." With these clean silhouettes, the lines and proportions need to look totally natural and perfect, which chimes with my tastes. Beautiful lapels, a good fit – I love that. I started out in Akris when I had to do an internship after my apprenticeship to qualify for textile college and I met Lu Künast, the head of what was then the coats and jackets atelier in Zurich. She was a real personality and played an important role in my professional development as a pattern-maker at Akris. People like that in a company influence generations of employees. She was also very important for Albert.

Manuela Lüthy-Schneider, Knitwear Designer
With Akris since: 2002

First of all, my team and I try to understand what Albert wants to achieve. His input often comes from the fabrics. We prepare stitches, work on swatches, order the yarns. I really like working with structures, such as the little trapezoids that are knitted in, intarsia and jacquards. Knitting is very sustainable because everything is knitted in shape. There's no waste.
You need expertise, professional skills, a great deal of technical knowledge. You should be rather self-confident and tenacious. If a proposal that convinces me isn't accepted, I'll have another go later from a different angle. Working with Albert is the most wonderful part for me, because he has a unique sense for the material. We can really pick from the full breadth of possibilities. And we can also become very involved in the creative side of things. You just have to take the plunge and stick with it.
For me, the current collection is always my favorite. When one collection is finished, I start looking forward to the next one.

WHOLE CLOTH STRET

Silke Söllner, Pattern-Maker for Coats and Casual Jackets
With Akris since: 1998

Akris found me through a recruitment agency. It took two attempts. The first trial was on a rainy November day. At that point, I didn't want to make a decision. Five months later, Akris asked if I wanted to come back in April. I enjoyed two spring days in the house with beautiful weather, in a very attractive city near striking natural landscapes. Primarily, of course, I was impressed by what Akris did and how; by the craftsmanship and the willingness to try something new.

My focus is on jackets and coats and everything related to new volumes, new silhouettes. It's a kind of volume-driven language that we devise. I appreciate being free to do my work, the trust shown towards me. All the input and ideas that come from my colleagues, how efficient we can be and the new things that emerge. We wouldn't be able to work like this otherwise. The young colleagues have a different way of developing a design. Their quality yardsticks relate to something else, a different kind of modernity.

Cornelia Hefti-Dörrer, Pattern-Maker for Blouses and Tops

With Akris since: 1981

There are days when I think to myself: It is getting really a bit crazy now. But after forty years, I still enjoy being at work every day. You have to put your heart into it, feel a connection, and then the work will never get boring. A lot of that is thanks to the team I work with here. In our collections, the blouse is usually the smallest item you wear, so I'm thrilled when I see it styled with a suit or a skirt in a show or a lookbook. What I find most intriguing is deciding how to make up a sample piece, thinking about what could work well and what might not. We use all our skills and passion to make women look beautiful in Akris in every size, not just in size 34.

Manfred Sperrer, Pattern-Maker for Pants
With Akris since: 2005

At the very beginning, I met Ute Kriemler, Albert's and Peter's mother, in the showroom in Düsseldorf, Germany. I was invited to get familiar with the collection before I even started to work for Akris. That was when I first experienced her warmth and how she dealt with people. It was lovely to know someone like her was there, embodying the spirit of the house. It left a truly powerful impression on me. Pants are rather particular because they are one of the few garments that fit very snugly on the body. It very much depends on the individual physiognomy – the pelvis, the hips, the waist, the butt, the posture and how high the heels are on your shoes.
Developing various styles of pants is always based on Albert's input. Very few people have as precise an eye as he does. I find it fascinating to create garments that are a perfect transposition of his wishes.
If Albert says on a Thursday before a show that he needs something by Friday, we usually manage it. There's nowhere else that you would find ideas being realized at such speed, with the energy that the team develops in those situations. That is also the Akris spirit.

Caroline Brokmann, Accessories Designer
With Akris since: 2008

I'm still learning from and with my team every day. Some of the leather artisans and pattern-makers have been involved in developing high-quality leather goods for decades and I benefit from their wealth of experience. The depth and concentration involved in the development processes are unique. At Akris there is always a "reason why," a deeper meaning, a significance. If you are interested, you can discover a huge world here. Albert says, "It's not just about wanting to do something; you have to have the skills to do it, too." You need to be smart, ready for action, reliable. You must have commitment, initiative, must be willing to say, "I'm going to do it right now," to keep on learning. And to stand up for your own point of view.

Feliciano Pisaturo, Head of Sewing Atelier

With Akris since: February 2002

I am Italian and come from near Salerno; in my family everyone is a tailor. When I applied, Akris was looking for a tailor for the double-face atelier. There were already some Italians working there. I liked it right away. I specialize in bespoke and handmade work. That's what I love. If Albert wants a change very shortly before the show, I sew and iron the garment by hand. That makes it possible to do much more beautiful and precise work, to get the fit right and make any adjustments. That's something a machine will never be able to do. Dexterity is a crucial skill in my profession and it's not a gift that everyone has. I'm still working on spotting as fast as possible who can bring that to the team. My most emotional moment here so far was seeing the LED dresses in the Thomas Ruff collection on the catwalk. We spent so many hours working on those LED pieces, invisibly welding the electrified thread while sewing a perfect evening gown that chimed with the inspiration in the art. It was pure craftsmanship.

Susanna Welte, Head of Cutting

With Akris since: 1993

It is nothing short of amazing in this day and age to see a family business celebrating its centenary, particularly in the textile industry, which has undergone such enormous changes. That is down to the two brothers. I like the challenge of making things work even when it seems impossible at first. And that there is always a way to find solutions. Even with thirty-nine years of cutting experience, you always run up against a limit and have to consider how to solve the riddle. You also experience failures and realize that the next time you would do it differently. The transformation of the textile industry has led to a shortage of professionals, with more and more companies closing down. That affects the fabrics and the quality, for you need craftsmanship to make these exquisite pieces. What has happened to the weavers and their knowledge and skills? You also need dyeing experts, not just someone to stand by a machine and press a button when a red light comes on. Even if you are cutting out a pattern, you need to have learnt how to do it.

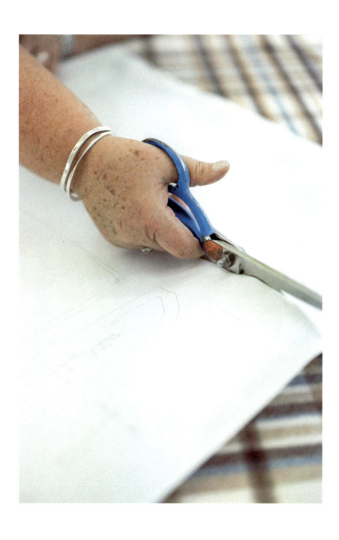

Coat Puller print on silk/outdoor alpaca double-face

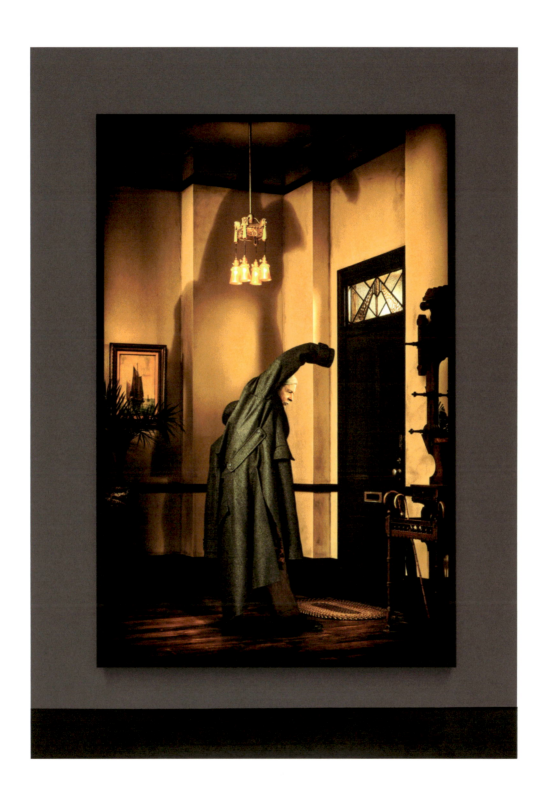

A WOMAN IN A COAT WITH A BAG, Palais de Tokyo   A code of coats. There is no way to look more sophisticated and poised than in a great coat. I was already working on a coat-only collection when I saw Canadian artist Rodney Graham's work *Coat Puller* (pictured). It sparked the idea of a collection about the intuitive move when a woman slips into her coat, grabs her bag and leaves the house. Rodney traveled to Paris and we were both excited about our grand finale: six models revealing the step-by-step images of his series *Der Mantelanzieher*, unfolding on the backs of their coats.

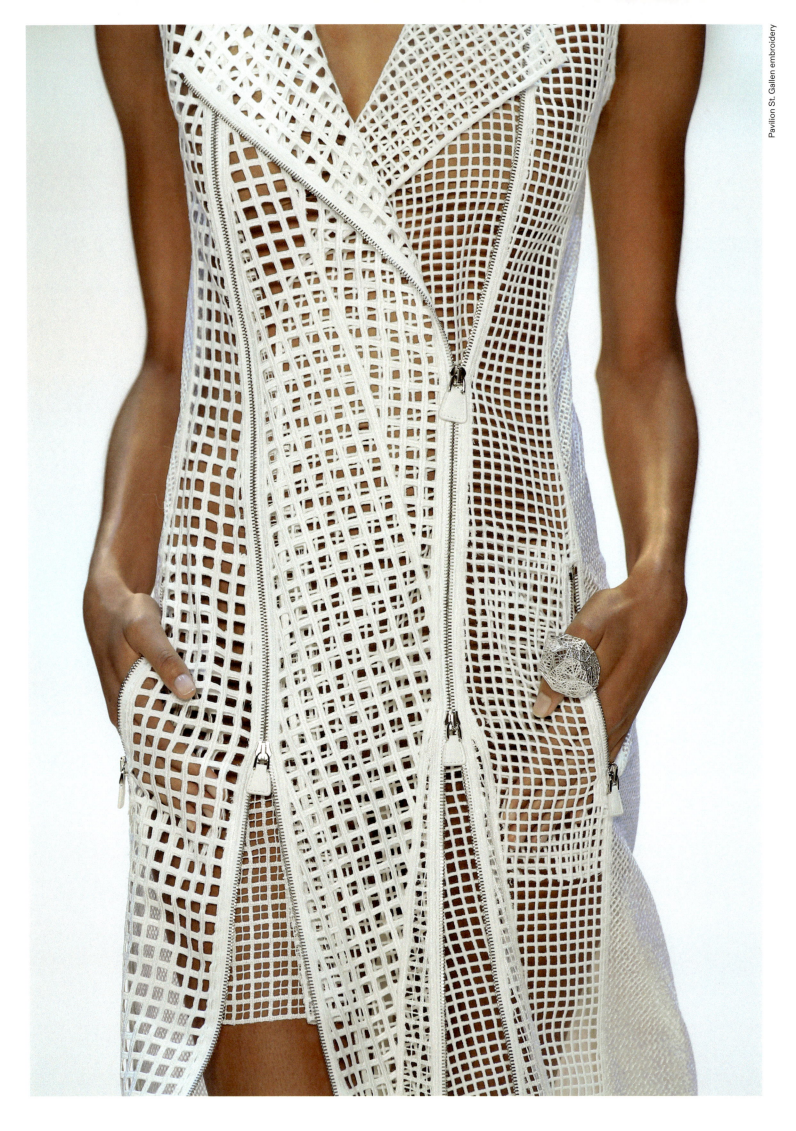

ALBERT KRIEMLER × SOU FUJIMOTO, Grand Palais Working with Japanese architect, and friend, Sou Fujimoto was one of my most memorable collaborations. When I went to London in 2013 to see his Serpentine Gallery Pavilion (pictured), I suddenly had this strong feeling of something great and new. In Sou's work, I recognize a desire to comprehend and create volume, space and room for people, to intertwine nature and construction, to work with transparency and opaqueness: all things that feel familiar to me. I visited him in Tokyo and saw him sketching in his signature red ink. When he came to Paris, he was as excited as I was about the reconstructed version of his House N on the catwalk.

Forest of Music cotton embroidery, cotton gabardine

Albert Kriemler × Sou Fujimoto

Red Ink cotton tweed bouclé, Serpentine Sketch embroidery on Cool Wool

Portrait reversible cashmere knit (with intarsia), silk crêpe georgette

ALBERT KRIEMLER × GETA BRĂTESCU, Pavillon Ledoyen   The magnetism of Geta. In her drawings, there are dancing lines, sensuous lips and twinkling eyes. The work of Romanian multimedia artist Geta Brătescu just makes you smile. When I visited her in her studio in Bucharest, she said: "Art exists to bring joy to our life. But it is a serious game," which can also be said about fashion. We worked with closures inspired by her *Magnets in the City* photomontage and flat plissé soleil, an innovative feat, for a fluid movement. Her joie de vivre infused a collection full of life, light and humor.

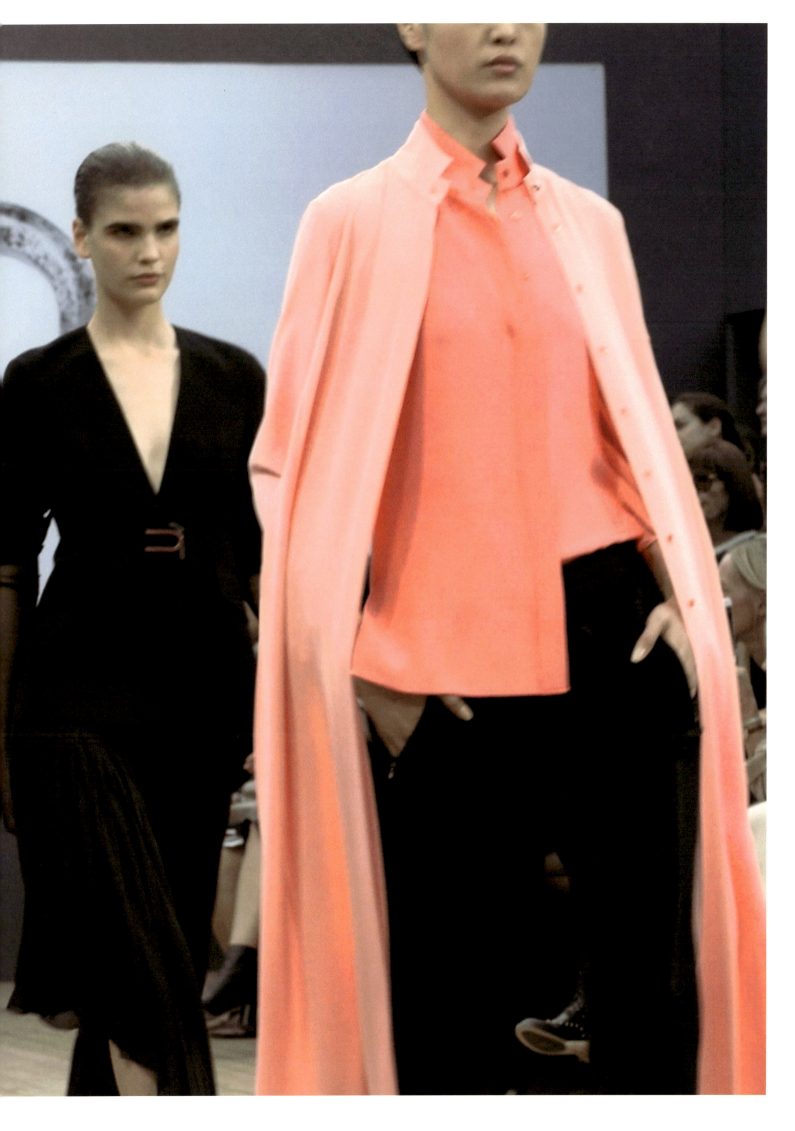

Magnets in the City print on silk plissé soleil

Albert Kriemler × Geta Brătescu

The Artist Collaborations

Albert Kriemler has established a unique base of mutual respect and trust with some of the most important contemporary artists whose works he translates into his collections

By Jessica Iredale

A deep, personal interest in art developed in Albert Kriemler as an extension of his love of architecture. He took the knowledge and appreciation of Adolf Loos and Robert Mallet-Stevens gleaned from his uncle, an architect who introduced him to the world of finessed, practical structure, and applied it to art. Beginning in the mid-1990s, Albert started casually attending Art Basel in Switzerland. "I wasn't even thinking of buying," he said. "It was just to form an opinion."

He would peruse the fair for a few days near closing time, preferring to tour on his own and rely on gut reaction rather than the guidance of a gallerist or curator. "It's always in my stomach," said Albert. After a few years, he was drawn to Paul Thek's sense of color and began collecting him, as well as purchasing an unknown piece by Le Corbusier and various works by Thomas Ruff.

From the time Albert started showing Akris on the Paris runways in 2004, artistic and architectural references became thematic parameters for his collections. The early runway shows incorporated the work of Swiss artist Félix Vallotton, Giorgio Morandi, Herzog and de Meuron and Ian Hamilton Finlay. A decade into Akris's tenure during Paris Fashion Week, Albert decided to take a more personalized approach to his artistic vision. He approached Ruff to do a hands-on collaboration for the Fall/Winter 2014 collection. "I called and said, 'Thomas, I have admired your work for years now,'" Albert said. "'I have always thought one day I would like to design a collection with your inspiration. What do you think about it?' And he said, 'I have no idea. Come see me and we will discuss.'"

"The process was, for me, really very simple," said Ruff, who recalled Albert flying into Dusseldorf to select the seven photographs from the Cassini, Stars, ma.r.s., and Night series as well as the digital photograms that he wanted to work with. "I sent him the high-res files and after two months he showed up with the first fabrics." Working with Ruff's photographs pushed Albert to upend his process. Typically, he would choose fabric first, but in this case the print led him to develop a new double-layered raincoat that was 3-D printed on the inside and outside with an interpretation of an image from Ruff's 3-D ma.r.s. series. The series consists of digitally altered images of the surface of planet Mars originally generated by a NASA orbiter.

As for Ruff, "I was more than surprised," he said. "Albert transformed these photographs into something completely different. It became his artwork, I would say."

In Albert's words, "That print from outer space wrote history. It landed on the shoulders of reggae legend Lee Perry on the cover of *Arena Homme+*, the first time one of my designs was featured on the cover of a men's fashion magazine."

"I did not have any hesitations. I'm a curious person. My work is also sometimes about appropriation. I pretty often use images from other authors and transform them into my art. I trusted Albert completely, and told him he should do whatever he wanted." – Thomas Ruff

Thomas Ruff and Albert Kriemler in
Ruff's studio in Düsseldorf

Imi Knoebel and Albert Kriemler in
Knoebel's studio in Düsseldorf

Albert's approach to artist collaborations has become a definitive aspect of Akris's runway collections. His way of translating an artist's work into a print, a palette, embroideries and intarsias preserves the integrity of the artist and their work while transforming it into sublime fashion through fit, imagination and highly considered technique. The final garment transcends the two-dimensional and becomes living art that interacts with the body. Albert's methodology and respect for the artist has lured the art-world and architecture elite, including Sou Fujimoto (Spring/Summer 2016), Carmen Herrera (Spring/Summer 2017), Rodney Graham (Fall/Winter 2017), Geta Brătescu (Spring/Summer 2019), Imi Knoebel (Spring/Summer 2021) and Reinhard Voigt (Fall/Winter 2022).

It's the combination of Albert's soft, personal touch, genuine interest in art, sense of proportion and refined eye that have cultivated a mutual admiration and trust between him and the artists and creators he has worked with. "Albert doesn't talk to me like a businessman but as an artist, which is what he is, and on that level there is a lot of mutual understanding and admiration," said photographer and director of films and music videos Anton Corbijn, who has twice collaborated with Albert. The first occasion was to direct a video of the Spring/Summer 2021 collection, inspired by the work of artist Imi Knoebel, a dear friend of Corbijn. The second was in 2021, when he was enlisted to shoot the collection in St. Gallen. Until then, he was unfamiliar with Akris. "It is always an adventure when you dive into something you know little about," Corbijn said. "To see Albert's thought process and follow it from his mind to the atelier to the models wearing the final result was wonderful."

> "Since the clothes were based on Imi Knoebel's paintings, I thought it would be great to set the story inside one of his installations and use the colors of his paintings as changing lights over the set. So there were always visual connections, whichever way you looked. Then I choreographed it a little and it became quite a fun little film piece." – Anton Corbijn

"Surprise" is a word often invoked by Albert's artistic collaborators when they see how he marries their specific vision with his.

Sou Fujimoto had never entertained the idea of doing a fashion collaboration before Albert approached him after falling in love with his Pavilion at the Serpentine Gallery in London. He was impressed by Albert's quiet passion and thorough knowledge of architecture. In their second meeting, Albert brought him a prototype of a fabric he intended to use to translate Fujimoto's vision into the collection. "Then for the first time, I understood that the constructiveness of architecture and coexistence of nature and artifacts, which are the characteristics of my architecture, can be translated onto the fabric level," Fujimoto said. "It was a big surprise."

> "It was an experience that made my team and myself realize the characteristics and meanings

Albert Kriemler and Reinhard Voigt in the atelier in St. Gallen

Albert Kriemler and Sou Fujimoto in the architect's studio in Tokyo

that our architecture had developed but we didn't recognize by ourselves. I think it was a journey to introspection by being exposed to an outside perspective. We saw unexpected commonalities. But also real characteristics that distinguish each field were vividly evident. It wasn't just about the fabric. The fabrics become clothes, and the model walking on the runway in these clothes, this movement, created a surprise that cannot be found in architecture. It was also a wonderful experience to see the elegance, delicacy and lightness embodied in all of the clothes designed by Albert, going from tranquility to dynamism from moment to moment." – Sou Fujimoto

Tony Bechara, a longtime friend of Carmen Herrera's and an artist himself, recalled how Albert approached Herrera after seeing her works in the first exhibition of the new Whitney Museum of American Art in New York City. "Carmen is famous for having said, 'I never met a straight line I didn't love,'" said Bechara. "'Keep it simple' was her philosophy of life. If you look at Albert's design, there's an element of that. His work is very elegant, very stylistically simple." Bechara arranged the meeting between Albert and Herrera, who was 101 years old at the time. "They met. They liked each other," said Bechara, who remembers the collaboration as one of a mutual give and take. "Albert was very respectful, loving and generous with her. And she was very intrigued that he was interested."

When Albert presented Herrera with the samples based on her Blanco y Verde series, "We were all surprised," Bechara said. "The green and white dress with a long slice of green across a field of white – Carmen was very pleased with the result." Her work featured prominently in Akris's Spring/Summer 2017 collection, staged in New York City at the famous Lever House building in September of 2016, coinciding with the opening of her first solo exhibition *Lines of Sight* at the Whitney.

"Albert was extremely respectful of the work. He wasn't going in there to just steal an image and then pull it and push it and come up with something that looked like Carmen. He was very, very focused on the piece, the art, Carmen's art." – Tony Bechara on behalf of Carmen Herrera

"Surprisingly easygoing" was how Rodney Graham described working with Albert for Akris's Fall/Winter 2017 collection. "It was a learning experience." For a collection based on coats, Albert had chosen to work with Graham's *Der Mantelanzieher*, and *Coat Puller*, which is a loose translation of the German word *Mantelanzieher*. The pieces are based on a sculpture of a man putting on a coat by the German sculptor Ernst Barlach. Graham was interested in capturing the shape a coat makes when you put it on and the "sometimes slightly absurd moments that a camera could catch." Albert used *Coat Puller* for the linings of a reversible Alpaca hooded coat and a tweed coat, while *Der Mantelanzieher* appeared on the back of six looks for the show's finale.

With Carmen Herrera in her studio in New York

Rodney Graham and Albert Kriemler at
Galerie Rüdiger Schöttle in Munich

With Geta Brătescu in her studio in Bucharest

When Graham spoke to Albert on the phone about the idea of collaborating, "I just intuitively trusted him," said Graham. "Of course, I was excited about the idea of working in a fashion context. I like to see my work in a different context. It was an opportunity for me to try something different, a kind of adventure." For him, it wasn't a difficult decision, it was enjoyable.

> "This is a little bit different from my work, which is collaborative to a degree. Here, I saw the backstage of a fashion show, everybody being busy doing different things. My shoots are of course not so big, but they are collaborative."
> – Rodney Graham

Marian Ivan, Geta Brătescu's longtime gallerist at the Ivan Gallery in Bucharest, hesitated when he heard Albert was proposing a fashion collaboration. "You knew when Geta didn't like someone," Mr. Ivan said. "She was polite, but she would keep the distance." When Albert arrived in Bucharest, however, they were completely simpatico, and Ivan recalled that Brătescu was impressed by Albert's eye for things that often went unnoticed. Specifically, *The Portrait*, a yellow collage featuring two big eyes and lips, which became the premise for a handbag in the Akris collection. "Geta really loved that collage and she was very fond of it, but not many people appreciated it," Ivan said.

> "[Albert] would pay attention to things that normally curators or gallery people or media people wouldn't notice immediately."
> – Marian Ivan

The yellow face collage and *Magnets in the City*, a photo-montage from 1974, became key works from Brătescu's oeuvre that Albert used in the collection. *Magnets in the City* is one of her strongest and most important works; it's also a very political work. Albert remembers how Brătescu asked him specifically to work with this image. "It was a bit risky, but in the end it was strong. It was powerful. He had quite a vision," Ivan said.

Brătescu passed away just two weeks before the Akris show in late September. Albert visited her at her Bucharest studio a final time in May 2018, showing her samples of the printed fabrics for the collection and a prototype of the collage bag. "It was like giving life to the work in a different way," said Ivan. "Especially with the yellow collage because Geta liked that that color so much. When he showed her how he printed it on a scarf, she was so happy."

ALBERT KRIEMLER × CARMEN HERRERA, Lever House, New York   When visiting the Whitney Museum of American Art, I first saw *Blanco y Verde*, a striking off-white plane with a green arrow-shaped triangle by Cuban-American artist Carmen Herrera. I met Carmen on May 31, 2016, which happened to be her 101st birthday. Immediately, the idea to show the collection in New York came up. Her abstract, geometric lines and dazzling colors captured my mind and heart. We translated them into breezy caftans, shirt dresses and sheaths.

Orange and Red print on crêpe marocain plissé

286   Albert Kriemler × Carmen Herrera

Venetian Red, White and Black print on organza

Albert Kriemler × Carmen Herrera

Cassini 02 print on wool double-face, wool crêpe double-face

ALBERT KRIEMLER × THOMAS RUFF, Grand Palais   In 2012, I saw a retrospective of Thomas Ruff's works at Munich's Haus der Kunst, and I knew that I wanted to do a collection with him at some point. Two years later, with the celebration of my tenth year in Paris, seemed to be the perfect moment. Thomas often works with existing generic images and transforms them using the most advanced technologies. This collection not only took my photo prints to a new dimension, it changed the way I work with artistic inspirations. Thomas and I met every month in his studio in Düsseldorf, reviewing sketches, fabrics and pieces, and I developed embroideries with LED lights inspired by his Stars series. They were our grand finale and they made their way into museum collections.

Night print on wool double-face

Fall/Winter 2014

ALBERT KRIEMLER × IMI KNOEBEL, A film by director Anton Corbijn   I strive for ease in each piece I design, for a feeling of just-rightness in its appearance: a key concept I discovered in the work of German artist Imi Knoebel. His humbleness and sense of color stunned me. He lets color shine. On one of my visits to his studio in Düsseldorf, we discussed his *Raum 19* and its extension *Batterie*, a giant phosphorescent block. It became our mutual delight and a wonderful metaphor for a moment in darkness to work on glow-in-the-dark fabrics. Anton Corbijn had the idea to bathe my collection in Imi colored lights, and it turned out to be one of my most inspired partnerships to date.

Lamb nappa leather, Ohayo print on silk crêpe de chine

Albert Kriemler × Imi Knoebel

Spring/Summer 2021

Blue Angel print on silk georgette

Kinderstern print on silk jersey and silk crêpe de chine | Cotton jersey cutout patchwork, Kinderstern print on silk crêpe de chine

Acknowledgments

Just as the master artisans in the studio play a vital role in creating our collections, so too do the advisors and people who contribute ideas, whether it be in management or from the wings, provide the foundation for the Akris success story and help shape a healthy, forward-looking company. We are most grateful to all of them. We should like specifically to thank Ernst Wegmann, Wolf-Dieter Lang, Corinne Kunz, Reiner Hämmerle and Spela Lenarcic, for they represent this spirit and have astutely headed the teams in charge of finances, production, design, coordination and corporate identity with us for decades. A particularly heartfelt thank you to them.

All Akris team members deserve our gratitude. The secret of our long journey in the perpetually changing global fashion world lies in our constancy and our love of detail – in St. Gallen and in our sites throughout Europe, Asia and the United States. What has come to seem natural and self-evident, *selbstverständlich*, to us in our daily work, is actually quite extraordinary and is something that has evolved from St. Gallen over a hundred years.

The contents of this book, developed by an inspired team with great attention to detail, bears witness to that. It pays tribute to Akris's history and looks to the future.

We should also like to thank those outside the house who have shown enormous personal commitment in supporting the research for this book, particularly Dr Valerie Steele, the director of The Museum at FIT in New York for her advice and friendship and Dr Ernst Ziegler for his research in St. Gallen's municipal and cantonal archives.

Albert Kriemler and Peter Kriemler

Contributors

Iwan Baan is an architecture and documentary photographer based in Amsterdam. In his photography, Baan focuses on the connection between architecture, its inhabitants and the surrounding environment. Instead of isolating the built structure, he embeds it in history and context.

Daniel Binswanger studied philosophy and comparative literature in Berlin and Paris. He is a journalist and worked for many years as a cultural correspondent in Paris, first for *Weltwoche*, then for *DAS MAGAZIN*. He is the founder and co-head of online magazine *Republik*'s feature section and lives in Zurich.

Jessica Iredale is a writer and editor based in New York City. A former fashion critic for *Women's Wear Daily*, she is a frequent contributor to *The New York Times*, *The Wall Street Journal* and *Town & Country* among many other publications.

Albert Kriemler is the creative director and co-owner of Akris along with his brother Peter.

John Neumeier has been the director and chief choreographer of the Hamburg Ballett at the Hamburg State Opera since 1973. Since 1996, he has also been its artistic director. Under his leadership, Hamburg Ballett has become one of the leading German ballet companies.

Nicole Phelps is the global director of *Vogue* Runway and *Vogue* Business. She began her fashion career at *Women's Wear Daily* and *W Magazine* and spent five years at *ELLE* before becoming the executive editor of Style.com. In 2015, she joined *Vogue*, where she launched the Vogue Runway app, which won a Webby Award in 2018. She lives in Manhattan with her husband and son.

Anne Urbauer is a journalist, writer and communications consultant based in Munich, Germany.

Nicole Urbschat is the deputy editor-in-chief of Germany's independent fashion magazine, *Achtung – Zeitschrift für Mode*. A writer and editor based in Berlin, she was a founding member of *Qvest Magazine*, fashion director at *Flair Magazine* and contributor to other publications. She is currently overseeing the editorial content and cultural relations at Akris.

Roland Wäspe studied art and architectural history as well as East Asian art history at the University of Zurich. He has been the director of the Kunstmuseum St.Gallen since 1989. In this capacity he has organized numerous temporary exhibitions for the Kunstmuseum and Kunstverein St.Gallen with a focus on contemporary art.

Photographs and Credits

Akris – A Century in Fashion
Selbstverständlich

Edited by
Albert Kriemler and Peter Kriemler

Texts by
Daniel Binswanger, Jessica Iredale,
John Neumeier, Nicole Phelps,
Anne Urbauer, Nicole Urbschat,
Roland Wäspe

Executive editor
Anne Urbauer

Editorial advisor
Lars Müller

Project coordinator
Corinne Kunz

Image editing
Akris, Haller Brun

Photography
Iwan Baan

Design
Haller Brun, Amsterdam

Translation
Helen Ferguson,
Catherine Schelbert (Binswanger)

Copyediting
Sarah Quigley, Viola van Beek

Proofreading
Sarah Quigley

Lithography, Printing
robstolk, Amsterdam

Binding
Brepols, Turnhout

Akris Prêt-à-Porter AG
St. Gallen, Switzerland
www.akris.com

Lars Müller Publishers
Zurich, Switzerland
www.lars-mueller-publishers.com

ISBN 978-3-03778-707-6

Distributed in North America by
ARTBOOK | D.A.P.
www.artbook.com

Printed in the Netherlands

Designs for Movement

There are many collaborations between fashion designers and opera houses. The one that unites choreographer and ballet director John Neumeier and Albert Kriemler spans more than fifteen years. John Neumeier on an era of exploring aesthetic functionality to the extreme

Albert Kriemler's designs combine a clarity of form with practical function. Quite simply, he obviously believes that clothes are made for people and people must be able to move in them!

Dance involves extreme movements and thus demands clothes that accommodate these extraordinary challenges. It was precisely Albert's fusion of architectural structure with limitless mobility that attracted me to his art. His creations are "classic" – while at the same time completely new, contemporary, relevant and forward-looking. Ballet, I feel, should share these qualities. It is therefore important for me to work with a designer who not only draws well but understands cut, construction and, most importantly, what his collaborator desires to express. This includes accepting the fact that in making a ballet, the focus may shift, change or develop constantly during the practical work and experience of creation.

Albert is precise regarding how a dress should be cut. But, at the same time, he is always ready to change everything if his work does not define or complement what I, with my ballet, wish to express. It is this combination of professional, accurate craftsmanship and vision with the pragmatic willingness to achieve functional relevance that makes Albert Kriemler an ideal creative partner for me.

We are two people who, I believe, truly complement each other in our creative endeavors. Mutual respect is key to our collaboration which began in 2005 with the dances and costumes for the Vienna Philharmonic's New Year's concert. However, as in all our subsequent work together, Albert created not "costumes" but clothes for dancers. This humanizing aspect of the theatrical wardrobe concurs exactly with my own desire not to see "dancers" on the stage, but rather people who happen to be dancing. Later, we worked together in Hamburg on the ballets *Verklungene Feste* and *Josephs Legende* (2008) as well as *Turangalîla* in 2015. Anna Karenina's exclusive wardrobe was designed by Albert for my ballet of the same name in 2017 – produced as a co-production with the Hamburg Ballett, the Bolshoi Ballet and the National Ballet of Canada. Our latest collaboration was the *Beethoven Project II* in 2021 in Hamburg.

It is my sincere wish that this may not be the last of our harmonious works together.